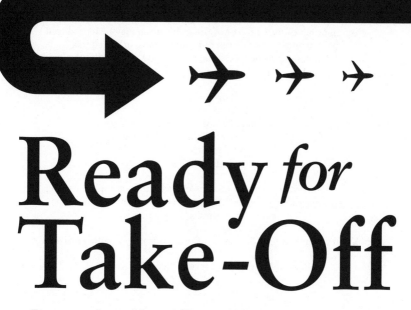

# Ready *for* Take-Off

## Preparing Your Teen With ADHD or LD for College

Theresa E. Laurie Maitland, PhD
and Patricia O. Quinn, MD

MAGINATION PRESS ● WASHINGTON, DC

AMERICAN PSYCHOLOGICAL ASSOCIATION

**This book is dedicated to the memory of Eleanor Laurie Sterling (1941–2005): Loving sister, mother, daughter, wife, and friend.**

Published by
MAGINATION PRESS
An Educational Publishing Foundation Book
American Psychological Association
750 First Street, NE
Washington, DC 20002

For more information about our books, including a complete catalog, please write to us, call 1-800-374-2721, or visit our website at www.apa.org/pubs/magination.

Book and cover design by Silverander Communications, Santa Barbara, CA

Printed by Worzalla, Stevens Point, Wisconsin

Library of Congress Cataloging-in-Publication Data
Maitland, Theresa L., 1947-
Ready for take-off : preparing your teen with ADHD or LD for college by Theresa E. Laurie Maitland and Patricia O. Quinn.
p. cm.

ISBN 978-1-4338-0891-3 (pbk. : alk. paper)

1. Learning disabled youth--Education (Higher)--United States.
2. Learning disabled youth--Education (Secondary)--United States.
3. College student orientation--United States. I. Quinn, Patricia O. II. Title.
LC4713.4.M35 2011
371.94--dc22

2010032113

First printing September 2010
10 9 8 7 6 5 4 3 2 1

# Contents

# Preface
## Flying Solo

You may have searched your local bookstore or online for information to help you better prepare your teen for college and been overwhelmed by the many books written for parents of college-bound high school students. You can find books to help your teen apply to college, get funding, know what to pack and know what to buy. You can find plenty of books designed to help parents let go of their teens. But few, if any books, exist to help teens get ready for life on their own.

That's right. *Life on their own.* College can be viewed as each teen's first, important solo flight in life. Although teenagers may have gone to a summer camp, studied abroad, or attended a boarding school, college is the first journey where they will have total freedom and responsibility with no copilot at their sides.

That might be the very reason you're losing sleep at night!

Given how different college is from high school, it stands to reason that many teens will experience some difficulties as they take off for college. High school just can't simulate all of the new experiences that college will offer.

And, because you have a son or a daughter diagnosed with attention-deficit/hyperactivity disorder (ADHD) or a learning disability (LD), you may be worrying much more about this upcoming solo flight than your neighbors are about their teens, or than you did about another child you sent off to college. Making appropriate choices, prioritizing time and tasks, solving new challenges, and then facing the increased academic demands in college can be much more problematic for teens with ADHD or LD. Plus you know far too much about the daily struggles and challenges your teen has had navigating her life, even with you around. You may even be wondering, "How will she make it without me?"

And that's why *Ready for Take-Off* was written, so that you and your teen can develop a Personalized College Readiness Program to use during your teen's remaining time in high school to prepare them for college life. By using the information in this guide you can:

- evaluate your parenting approach to make sure that you are helping and not hindering your teen's readiness;
- identify which skills your teen needs to develop to successfully transition to college;
- learn how to have empowering conversations with your teen; and
- create a readiness plan to allow your teen to slowly and systematically be ready for college.

Let's face it, no one would ever put a pilot in the cockpit and expect him to be ready for take-off or to fly solo without adequate preparation. Whether the transitioning teen is disabled or not, the truth is that how things turn out in college will depend largely on how prepared the teenager is for this new world. The Personalized College Readiness Program we will offer in this guide will help you prepare your teenager to face this new world and to transition smoothly to college life.

So, fasten your seat belt and let's go. Are you and your teen ready for take-off?

# Chapter 1
## The Challenges of Flying Solo in College

As one teen with attention-deficit/hyperactivity disorder (ADHD) put it after his first weeks in college, "Being in college is like being a kid in a candy store, but the owner has taken a permanent vacation. And even though I used to hate how my parents nagged me to get things done, I now realize that I don't know how to nag myself."

Each fall, several thousand recently graduated teens take off and attempt to fly solo in the unfamiliar world of college where more demanding classes and a host of other activities compete for their time and attention. With all of the freedoms found at college, no wonder the transition into this new environment can be extremely difficult. Learning to nag or parent yourself takes practice! The stark differences between high school and life in college are huge. Suddenly, a teen finds she is on her own and in need of an enormous amount of self-motivation and self-determination. Flying solo can be difficult even for the most prepared teenager, even ones who may have attended the toughest high school and balanced a full life with academics, sports, and hobbies with a minimum of support from teachers and parents.

### A Wake-Up Call

You've been dealing with your teen's ADHD or learning

disability (LD) for quite some time now and you're not naïve. While you fully expect that this transition to college will be difficult, you're hoping that what your teen has learned in high school—time management skills, organizational strategies, study habits—will be enough to get him through the first year and beyond. He's not a little kid anymore. Years of your reminders to eat right, to get enough sleep, and to take care of himself have sunk in, right? He even does his own laundry! So, you're hoping beyond hope that your teen will have what it takes to successfully weather any turbulence he encounters and be able to complete college.

But the hard truth is, not all teens who enter college may graduate on time or at all. Getting into college really is only half the battle! According to studies conducted by the National Center for Education Statistics (2000), only 53% of students diagnosed with disabilities, as compared with 64% of students without disabilities, received a college degree 5 to 6 years after enrolling. In other words, approximately 4 out of 10 students without any disabilities who go to the college may, at some point, leave college by choice or by necessity. These studies suggest that students with disabilities may graduate at an even lower rate than the already low graduation rate for students who don't have disabilities.

These students have all been accepted to college because they met the admissions standards and appeared to have what it takes to stay in school and succeed. So what can explain these dismal statistics? Why does this happen to so many qualified students? Did they forget to study? Socialize too much? Were they overreliant on their parents during high school?

Do they lack the necessary skills for life on their own? What's going on?

## Unexpected Turbulence for Transitioning Teens

While most teens look forward to the freedom that college offers, many are unprepared to take charge of their own lives. And this transition must happen literally overnight. In college, there is no adult supervision or built-in structure. Unlike high school, where adults typically enforce predictable daily routines, college life has a schedule that can vary from day to day with long periods of unstructured time that teens must learn to manage. As we have said before, teens must now make decisions and assume total responsibility for everything—when to sleep, eat, study, do laundry, see advisors, order and take medications, and so on.

Typically, there are no built-in structures to help a teen "stay on top" of her school work. With limited daily graded homework, infrequent tests, and big assignments that might not be due until the end of the semester, a student may just drift along until the deadline hits. In many cases, there may be no immediate consequence for skipping class or failing to take notes or to study regularly. To make matters even more complicated, campus life provides a smorgasbord of tempting activities to fill the unstructured time. Social and academic activities compete regularly for a student's time. The analogy of the kid in the candy store says it all. For some, their transition challenges can be directly related to a desire to "do it all" coupled with an inability to prioritize adequate time for classes and studying. With no adult around to set limits, teens can literally do anything they want.

On top of all this, academic expectations require refinements of old skills and development of new ones. Everything teens were used to in high school really does get turned upside down in college. The amount of work is much greater, and the strategies for learning are often unfamiliar. Instructors typically use a lecture approach rather than the interactive discussions teens were accustomed to in high school. Class size may be overwhelming at times, with several hundred students seated together in a large lecture hall or auditorium. In addition, college professors are typically content experts or researchers who may not have much exposure to principles of teaching and learning. Instantly, college students must become proficient at studying, making sense of class presentations, and comprehending hefty reading assignments that may or may not be directly discussed in class. They must immediately become active learners synthesizing large volumes of information, as well as detectives figuring out how to identify and organize the most important knowledge. Some teens have literally no practice with these more advanced study skills. During high school, they may only have learned how to do homework and study for weekly tests that required lower level knowledge, like memorizing new vocabulary and facts. In college only two or three exams may be given each semester, so students don't have a large margin for error or much time to figure things out.

And when things go wrong, students must seek out resources on their own. For many bright college students, using resources is a foreign concept. During high school, they lived in a world where teachers organized the lessons to facilitate learning and reached out to offer help when problems surfaced. Most teens never learned how to study, write a paper, or face a task they couldn't figure out. This "lone ranger" pattern often leads new college students to mistakenly view any struggles with learning as a sign of failure rather than normal adjustment issues to the college academic scene. They may be ashamed to admit they are confused, let alone tell anyone the truth about what is happening. Some students may have had parents who magically connected them to tutors or other resources when problems occurred without their involvement. And unless a teen went to a boarding school, he may never have had to deal with an emotion like homesickness or issues like roommate problems. At times, transitioning teens may refuse to seek help until it is almost too late because they don't know how or because they have difficulty accepting the fact that what they are doing isn't working.

## Veering Off Course With ADHD or LD

The good news is that the number of college students diagnosed with ADHD or LD has increased significantly in recent decades. However, despite having greater access to college, they may experience even greater technical difficulty than students who don't have these issues. Although little research exists on how these students are faring in college, what does exist paints a concerning picture. College students with ADHD or LD may have lower grade point averages (GPAs), get placed on probation more often, may take longer to graduate, and may even have lower graduation rates than students with other disabling conditions (Barkley, Murphy, & Fischer, 2007; D'Amico, personal communication, January 29, 2008; Heiligenstein, Guenther, Levey, Savino, & Fulwiler, 1999; Murray, Goldstein, Nourse, & Edgar, 2000; National Center for Education Statistics,

2003; Newman, Wagner, Cameto, & Knokey, 2009; Rabiner, Anastopoulos, Costello, Hoyle, & Swartzwelder, 2008; Vogel & Adelman, 1990a, 1990b, 2000; Vogel et al., 1998; Vogel, Leyser, Wyland, & Brulle, 1999; Wagner, Newman, Cameto, Garza, & Levine, 2005).

To investigate these issues more fully, we'll introduce some students with these disabilities whose first solo flights got off course. We'll spend the remainder of this chapter taking a closer look at some of the factors leading to college adjustment problems that appear to be directly related to ADHD and LD.

## Disability Laws and Requirements to Receive Services

Kristina went off to college accepting her special needs, and knowing that she would require services and accommodations to be successful. She was fortunate to have had her problems recognized early on and was diagnosed in third grade with learning disabilities that affected both her reading and writing skills. She was reevaluated periodically and continued receiving education services until she graduated from high school. Kristina took advantage of all the modifications the laws governing K–12 would allow, including meeting daily to receive individualized instruction from a special class teacher and receiving many modifications in her regular classes. Her IEP (Individualized Education Plan) allowed her unlimited time for tests, reduced assignments, and flexible deadlines when she had multiple tests or papers due at once. Her teachers did not count off for spelling errors when they graded her in class tests and assignments. As a result, Kristina excelled and developed a strong high school record that got her accepted into the college of her dreams. However, she was blindsided when she arrived at college and found out that she didn't automatically qualify for accommodations because her last psychoeducational report was over 3 years old. She had to spend most of the first semester of her freshman year without accommodations while she waited to be tested. Without extended time, she did very poorly on college exams. Once she was eligible for disability accommodations, she again was shocked to learn that her professors were not required to make many of the special modifications she had accessed in high school, such as modified assignments and flexible deadlines. She could get extended time for tests but not the unlimited time she was used to. She actually never monitored time on an exam until she got to college. She didn't have access to daily meetings with a learning specialist; instead she could see someone once a week for 30 to 60 minutes. Unfortunately, she barely made the grades to return to college for the second semester.

As Kristina discovered the hard way, the laws, resources, and modifications at the college level are very different from those available at the high school level. This creates a major disconnect between what parents and teens were used to and what actually exists in college. For example, college programs are mandated to make the environment accessible for students with disabilities by providing "reasonable accommodations." Giving accommodations such as extended time, notes, audiobooks, and so on are designed to "level the playing field" and make sure students can compete. There are no laws at the college level mandating that each student have an *individualized* plan or the delivery of evidence-based interventions that guarantee a student's success. Colleges are only required by law to offer generic accommodations.

In addition, colleges typically require recent documentation to demonstrate the impact of a disability. Unfortunately,
many teens like Kristina discover late in the game that they
do not have the type of documentation needed to be eligible
for accommodations and services at the college level. Parents
can't assume that if their teen has a diagnosis, an official
report of his disability, and a history of services, then he will
automatically qualify for accommodations or services in
college. They must plan ahead and know what the documenta-
tions guidelines are at the college their teen attends. The laws
governing colleges (Section 504 of the Rehabilitation Act of
1973 and the Americans With Disabilities Act of 1990) give
them the right to define their documentation guidelines. Most
colleges won't accept an IEP or a 504 plan (document stating a
student received accommodations), a Summary of Performance
(SOP), or an outdated psychological report. There is no consis-
tency in the documentation needed at the college level. The eli-
gibility requirements for accommodations and services at one
college may be totally different from those needed at another
college, even within the same state!

## Students With Disabilities Must Access Accommodations/Services

Abraham used very limited accommodations and support
during his years in school. He was not diagnosed with ADHD
until seventh grade and then only because of his distractibility, poor organization skills, and his inability to complete assignments on time. Medication had a positive impact on his
symptoms, but Abraham really hated taking it. He didn't
want to be different from his friends. When Abraham entered

high school, his parents fought to get him a 504 plan so he could have extra time on exams and access to a separate testing room. Unless his parents and teachers forced him to use these accommodations, however, Abraham didn't use them because he didn't like being asked questions by his friends about where he was during class tests.

Once Abraham was accepted into college, his parents wanted to make sure he could get all the accommodations and help he needed. During freshman orientation he grudgingly joined his parents in a visit to the Disabilities Services Office so that he could enroll and know how to access accommodations. But Abraham was not worried about his transition. He felt he would do well in college because he did so well in high school without much extra support. Despite all his parents' efforts to ensure that he had what he needed in college, Abraham had considerable difficulties because he didn't use the accommodations that were available to him. He ignored all the e-mail reminders about the deadlines to request accommodations from the Disabilities Services Office and didn't attend any of their orientation meetings. By the time a friend with ADHD convinced him to use accommodations, he was in dire straits. Eventually, right before final exams, Abraham made his first appointment to get accommodations, but by then his GPA had already been negatively  impacted and he was experiencing a great deal of stress. He actually had to withdraw from college before final exams and take a semester off to figure things out.

Much to Abraham's parents' dismay, they realized too late that in college, the responsibility for accessing services rests solely on the student. Many college students, including those with ADHD or LD, don't want to be different from their peers. Consequently, too many resist asking for help or receiving accommodations, and this further complicates their situation as they attempt to navigate the new world of college. In fact, a recent study found that only 39% of students with all types of disabilities who received special help in high school actually officially registered with the Disabilities Services Offices once in college (Cortiella, 2009). And not all of these students used the help available to them. Also, in far too many cases, students like Abraham have no experience being responsible for requesting accommodations, and this inexperience gets in the way. Oftentimes, parents and teens are used to the teachers being responsible for setting up everything at the start of the semester. Discovering that nothing happens in college until students take charge of their accommodations can be both surprising and frustrating. Not to mention that teens can't be forced to take this step.

## Academic Demands and Skill Deficits

Elena's reading disabilities were obvious at a very early age. She first received speech and language help in preschool because of her difficulty hearing and reproducing sounds and because she processed spoken information so slowly. When it came time to learn letters and sounds and to read, she experienced even more difficulty. She needed a great deal of daily help and special education services to "crack the code" and learn to read. With great determination, Elena conquered her high school honors classes by using audiobooks and the frequent reading and rereading of information. She just accepted the fact that her disability caused her to work harder than others students, and she willingly gave up many outside activities to get the grades she needed to be accepted into the college of her choice. Day 1 in college, she was hit with reading assignments in several of her classes that covered hundreds of pages. One week she had three tests and two 15-page papers due at the same time. In high school her IEP allowed her to modify assignments so that she could space them out. It quickly became apparent to Elena that she was falling behind, even with specialized reading technology providing audio versions of her assignments, and the help she received from a learning specialist in efficient study strategies. Elena just couldn't keep up and ended up at the university's counseling center one day with a panic attack. She received counseling and learned that she could still lighten her course load by dropping a class and was encouraged to find an extracurricular activity to give her life some balance. However, her GPA and her self-esteem had already been significantly affected.

As Elena's situation demonstrates, the academic skill deficits of students with ADHD or LD are often at direct odds with the academic expectations of college. Students must quickly adapt to the increased academic demands for learning and functioning independently that college requires. As a consequence of their disabilities, many students with ADHD or LD experience challenges in academics and often lack the skills to manage their attention, their emotions, and their time. Although students may learn strategies and techniques for managing these difficulties in high school, oftentimes these strategies won't work in college. Elena, like many students with learning disabilities, coped by accepting that she works more slowly. This approach can backfire when the volume of work increases exponentially at the college level and there aren't enough hours in a day to get it done working slowly. In addition, teachers in high school may frequently reduce assignments, delay deadlines, and give extra and unlimited time or alternative exams. Professors, however, do not have to alter their assignments, delay due dates, or modify their exams as part of their legal authority to define their course requirements.

## Too Much Help From Adults

Brendan was diagnosed with ADHD in first grade. His inattention, hyperactivity, and disorganization wrecked havoc in all areas of his life. His mother learned early on to "stay on top of" Brendan so he would remember what he needed to do at home and at school. While he did well in school, it was mainly because his mom, and at times his dad, did a lot of the planning and thinking to keep him together. Even in high school they had to run back to school regularly to get the books he forgot for homework. His teachers also played a part in keeping Brendan afloat. They suggested that he have another set of books at home to prevent him from having to come back to school and assigned him a study buddy to go over his assignments at the end of the day. Once he got home his parents sat with him to make up a schedule for homework, telling him what he would do when. They even had him do his homework at the dining room table to ensure he'd get it done. They imposed strict rules for homework time and restricted access to the computer and his phone. They made him do large assignments in increments that they planned out on a calendar. In addition, like so many individuals with ADHD, Brendan had trouble falling asleep and waking up. His parents took on this issue as their own, too! They would patrol at night to make sure he had "lights out" at an appropriate time and they would make sure he was up in the morning.

However, with all the planning and thinking his parents did, they forgot about one important thing: They weren't going to be in college with Brendan! So, needless to say, Brendan was not ready, and things quickly fell apart for him at college. Not because he had documentation that was too old; his was current. Not because he resisted asking for help; he did. And not because he read slowly; he read just fine. He was unprepared for college because the adults in his life gave him too much help. They had filled in all the gaps and self-management problems caused by his ADHD. Brendan became ineligible to return after his first semester.

As Brendan's story demonstrates, another key factor that affects the success of teens with ADHD or LD seems directly related to what has transpired in their lives and the day-to-day patterns and beliefs that the adults in their worlds employed. In our many years of dealing with young adults, we have found that parents and sometimes teachers unfortunately don't always think long term and may not fully appreciate the reality that teenagers will face at college. Instead, many adults, like those in Brendan's life, often fall into nonproductive patterns to help teens get through the many crises that arise each day in high school. As a result, few adults actually use the years of high school preparing teens to pilot their own lives.

It is all too common for many well-meaning parents and

teachers like Brendan's to literally think for teens with ADHD or LD. Deficiencies in the thinking skills needed for self-management are common in teenagers with these conditions. As you well know, teens with these challenges do have real difficulty planning and prioritizing what to do when and then actually doing what they say they are going to do. The ability to catch themselves when distracted and to put on blinders so they stay on track is typically very hard. These deficits can also cause teens to get lost in an emotional reaction and not see or think through a situation to solve a problem or make a decision about what is the best path to take. So caring adults may inadvertently deprive teens of the opportunities to develop these important higher level thinking skills—executive functioning skills—that will be needed to navigate college and eventually in life by continuously making their teen's decisions and solving their problems for them.

We've also seen what happens when adults let go and stop micromanaging their teens, only to discover that things fall apart. Instead of learning from mistakes like other children do, teens with difficulty thinking and managing on their own may become depressed and frustrated and react emotionally rather than think things through. At this point, parents tend to panic and are not able to let natural consequences play out for their teens. Unfortunately, when parents do all the thinking for their kids with ADHD or LD, parenting becomes piloting, and the teenager can become all too comfortable being a passenger in his or her life. This is a pattern that students like Brendan discover will backfire immediately in college.

## What's Next? A New More Productive Approach

While hearing the "bad news" in this chapter may have been difficult for you, be assured that we feel that teens with ADHD and LD can be and are successful in college. Their success, however, to a large degree depends on both their preparation and their self-determination as well as the college they choose to attend. But it can also depend on your parenting approach, your willingness to honestly evaluate your teen's readiness, and your being proactive in developing a plan to use during high school to help your teen be ready for take-off.

We have designed this guide so that parents like you can work with your teenagers to develop a Personalized College Readiness Program. Through the use of this guide, we believe that you can learn how to gradually move from being the sole pilot, to copiloting along with your teen. And then when it is time you can hand over the controls as your teen takes off for college, with you still remotely available through cell phone, e-mails, and text messaging to provide support and guidance. We believe, from our work with families and transitioning teens, that it is possible to put a Personalized College Readiness Program into place well before your son or daughter takes off for college. With such a program, your teen can practice being as independent as possible while still living in the shelter and support of your family. We also believe that with accurate information about how different college is from high school, more teens will come to college better equipped to handle the freedom and responsibility they find there. It is our hope that this guide will play an important role in reversing the current trend that leads many bright young people with ADHD or LD to leave college prematurely. Instead, we hope this guide can be used to help more teens with these differences come to college informed and better prepared to reach their goals and dreams.

# Chapter 2
## Who's Piloting the Plane?

As we've mentioned in Chapter 1, the parenting approach you choose can make a real difference in your teen's life and either increase or decrease her chances for success in college. Luckily, you still have time before your teen goes off to college to work on your approach. In this chapter, you will have an opportunity to take a critical look at the role you now play in the life of your son or daughter with attention-deficit/hyperactivity disorder (ADHD) or learning disability (LD). You will be encouraged to analyze your role and see if you are actually "piloting the plane" and enabling your teenager causing him to be overly dependent on you. Then in the next chapter we will share a new, more productive pattern: a coaching approach to parenting that will allow you to empower your teen to think and act for himself.

## Sound Familiar? Common Parenting Scenarios

Take a look at the following scenarios, which are modeled after real-life situations that many families living with teens with ADHD or LD encounter on a daily basis. Maybe these scenarios have already played out in your house! As you read each scenario, and see how the parent responds, consider what you would do if this situation happened to you.

### Tom and His Mother

It is almost midnight, and Tom, an 11th grader, whose ADHD

causes major organizational problems, comes barreling down the stairs in a panic. "Mom, I just remembered, I need to have a poster session about my science experiment for tomorrow morning at 9:00. I totally forgot about it because I didn't write it down in my planner. Since I can't drive alone this late at night, would you just run me to Wal-Mart, and help me get this done tonight?"

What happened next? Because she is worried about her son getting low grades that could stop him from getting into college, Tom's mother drops everything she is doing to drive him to Wal-Mart and stays up late into the night to help him make his posters.

## Kathy and Her Father

It's 7:00 a.m. and Kathy's father is pacing at the bottom of the stairs. He's heard the alarm go off, but Kathy obviously hit the snooze button again. There's no evidence that she's up. He thinks, "I know she stays up late to finish her work because she works slowly, but she's 15 years old! When is she going to learn to wake herself up?" Although he has told her a million times to be ready no later than 7:25, here it is another morning, where she is "pushing the envelope." Because there is no bus service, he drives Kathy to school again.

Knowing that Kathy takes so long to do her homework because of her reading disability, her father talks to his boss about delaying his starting time each day to avoid a battle with Kathy and let her sleep in a little.

## Heather and Her Mother

Heather's mom is cleaning up her daughter's bedroom and

finds a progress report. She shakes her head in disbelief. Even though Heather asked her to "stop checking on me and treating me like a baby, of course, I'm getting all of my work done!" she reads that Heather is missing several assignments. The IEP (Individualized Education Plan) states that Heather's special class teacher is supposed to check weekly to make sure all assignments are done. Her mom thinks, "I knew better than to stop checking on Heather daily. She just can't be trusted! I should have called her teachers, too." Heather promised that things would be different this year. But as her mom looks at the crumpled progress report, she thinks, "Nothing has changed!"

The next day Heather's mom gets angry at the teachers and demands to have an emergency IEP meeting and blames the teachers for not calling her to let her know that Heather has missed assignments.

## Christopher and His Mother

Christopher's mother returned to work as a teacher and can't "spoil him" like she used to. He's a senior who will soon be on his own, so she set the expectation for him to make his own breakfast, pack his lunch, and do his laundry. Given his ADHD and learning disabilities, she's worried about how he'll make it at college. During the summer he learned how to cook and do laundry. Now that school has started she wants him to "own" these daily chores. But she feels guilty because he's running out the door without eating breakfast and without packing lunch. She peeks in his room and sees dirty clothes strewn all over the floor. She wonders what she should do because he obviously isn't taking over these chores.

Out of guilt and concern that he can't do all of these things because of his disabilities, Christopher's mom decides to go back to packing his lunch, making his breakfast, and picking up his dirty clothes when she does the family's laundry.

## Ella and Her Papers

It's dinner time and Ella is near tears because she has papers due in several classes next week and she hasn't started writing them. She's done the research but has avoided writing because it is so difficult for her. Ella is begging her mother to intervene and ask to have the deadlines for the papers moved ahead a couple of weeks. Ella's mother has mixed feelings about this. Although the IEP states that Ella's allowed flexible deadlines, she also knows that her daughter has been on the computer chatting with friends and failed to tell her about these papers until tonight.

Feeling sorry for Ella because of her writing disability, Ella's mom immediately agrees to call the school and demands that the due date for all papers be moved as her IEP states.

# What's a Parent to Do?

In each of these situations, the parent must determine how to respond. That response can either promote change, moving teenagers toward independence, or keep teens locked in a pattern that can reinforce dependency on the adults in their lives. The parental responses in these situations may seem exaggerated, but they are all too real and are likely to backfire if things don't change before these teens leave home.

## Enabling: A Nonproductive Pattern

A parent's well-meaning actions and desire to help their teen be successful and lead a stress-free life can result in a parenting response we refer to as *enabling*. Enabling is doing something for someone else that she should be able to and needs to do for herself. Enabling is a term used frequently in the field of alcohol and drug addiction to describe the behavior of a family member who rescues the addicted individual from the consequences of his own self-destructive behavior. In a more general sense, it can also be used to describe the act of rescuing anyone who is caught up in a self-destructive act.

To avoid conflict, parents may choose to bail kids out, let them off the hook, accept their excuses, create new excuses, or blame other people. In many instances, parents inadvertently fall into enabling simply because it is easier and it works, in the short run at least. In the busy lives of today's families, parents and teens often aren't even thinking about whether these patterns are really going to help the teen navigate life on her own. They are just trying to get through the day!

When any parent consistently chooses enabling responses, they can prevent their teen—even one without disabilities—from learning the important lessons that will be necessary for him to function on his own in college. However, if parents consistently enable a teen with learning, attention, and emotional challenges, they may not realize that they may be setting the wheels in motion for the teen to face considerable difficulties later in college and in life. Unlike teens without these differences, teens with ADHD or LD may not just figure things out when they are on their own or learn quickly from the mistakes they make transitioning to the many new demands in college.

## Enabling and Parenting Children With ADHD or LD

Could you actually see yourself responding like the parents in the above scenarios? Did Brendan's story in the last chapter sound eerily familiar? If so, don't feel embarrassed or guilt ridden! We understand how the differences that children with ADHD or LD have can actually entice the adults in their lives to do the hard work of thinking for them. Because these young people really do have difficulty with focusing, planning, implementing a plan, solving problems, managing themselves, and making decisions, parents and teachers may unconsciously fall into the trap of structuring the world for these teens and telling them what to do, reminding, nagging, and supervising as a way to prevent things from going awry. Oftentimes when adults do "let go," they learn quickly that their teenagers with ADHD or LD don't automatically pick up the slack, and things can quickly spiral out of control. So many adults stay stuck in patterns of enabling, micromanaging their teenagers because they don't know what else to do.

In addition, parents of children with learning, attention, and emotional disabilities may also become enablers because of the myriad difficulties they encounter raising a child with such significant differences. Sometimes, when their children are younger, parents pick and choose which battles to fight because there are so many. These can range from not being able to get dressed and out the door in the morning to having trouble sitting through a meal, or forgetting homework and important school announcements, flying off the handle at the slightest frustration, being picked on by teachers and other kids, and getting low grades despite doing more work than other students. Also, the inconsistency in their child's functioning and the battles of wills that can occur when rules and limits are enforced make it hard for parents to know when they should let go or when they really do need to be supportive.

When parents continue to take charge, fix things, or dictate what to do, this pattern of enabling can become counterproductive and actually hinder raising successful, independent young adults. We fully understand that deciding how to respond is even more complicated when teens have legitimate disabilities that make it difficult for them to complete various tasks. When should parents pitch in and help and when should they back off and let teenagers face the natural consequences of their choices? What really is helpful to do in situations like those described above? Obviously, the answer to each of these questions is not a simple one. No rulebooks are available to tell you exactly what to do.

While no parent is perfect, it is important that you not become part of the problem and take over "piloting the plane." If parents consistently fall into a pattern of enabling, this can result in teens shirking their responsibilities, manipulating others, and thus actually reinforcing behavioral patterns that others won't tolerate and that won't work later on in life. Nor would it be helpful for you to always push for changes to be made in the environment while not working simultaneously with your teen to help him take responsibility for his choices. Take the time now to pinpoint any parenting patterns you may have fallen into that won't be helpful in the long run. Then use the information found in the next chapter to help you choose patterns that will contribute to your teen learning the important skills that will be the key to her success in the future.

## Further Analysis: Enabling Questionnaire

Take a moment and think about the responses you were con-
sidering as you read each of the situations listed earlier to
become more aware of your pattern of reacting. How often
were your responses similar to those listed in the above examples?
Did you tend to come up with a solution to these situations
that could inadvertently encourage the teenager to do the same
thing again? Did you opt for responses that would give you
more work or responsibility than the teen in the situation?
Did you tend toward solutions that required changes in the
environment but did not promote responsibility and thinking
skills in the teen? What are you learning about your patterns?

Read through the following questions to learn more about
whether you tend to enable your teen. Think about each situation
and tally your answers as "never," "sometimes," or "often." This
should give you an idea on which areas may need more immediate attention as you work to adjust your response patterns.

- Do you find yourself worrying about your teenager's life and
  disabilities in ways that dominate your time?

- Do you think more about your teen's life and problems than
  he does?

- Do you find yourself figuring out solutions to your teenager's
  problems rather than letting her solve things for herself?

- Do you give solutions rather than ask open-ended questions?

- Do you ever find yourself doing your teenager's chores
  and tasks or do you spend lots of time nagging about his
  responsibilities?

- Do you make excuses for your teenager's behavior, claiming that such behaviors are a result of her disabilities and she can't help it?

- Do you find yourself giving your teenager rewards (money, privileges, etc.) because you feel sorry for him and want a way to reduce his pain?

- Do you find yourself feeling angry and resentful that your teenager doesn't follow through with your advice because you think you really do know what she needs to do?

- Do you feel protective of your teenager, even though he is growing up and quite capable of taking care of himself?

- Do you wish that other people would change their behaviors and attitudes to make things easier for your teenager or do you tend to blame others for your teenager's problems?

- Do you feel manipulated by your teenager but choose to ignore these feelings?

- Do you make yourself more available to your teenager at the expense of your own energy and time commitments?

## What Is Your Role?

We've provided two tools in this chapter to help you determine if you are part of the problem and responding in ways that could be preventing your teenager from being ready for college. The scenarios and the enabling questionnaire may have started you thinking, but here are some other ways to help you become more aware of your patterns.

**Ask others for feedback.** Gather your courage and ask your partner, your teen, or your friends if they see you doing anything that might be discouraging your teen's independence.

Hearing their answers might be hard, but the best information could come from those who see you in action. Want to be really courageous? Ask your teen's teachers!

**Keep a journal for several days or a week.** Commit to writing about the interactions you had with your teen for a full week. Keep track of times you got involved in talking with your teen. List the facts. What was going on? What did you say and do? What did she say and do? Keep a running log of these situations. After making several entries, step back and read each with specific questions in mind. What role am I playing when I interact with my teen? Am I providing the solutions to problems or asking questions? How much of my energy is taken up in helping my teen function?

**Reflect on what you've learned.** Before moving on to the next chapter, take some time to reflect on what you learned about yourself. It is possible that you discovered that sometimes you do respond in ways that are enabling. Think about the following questions: If you are enabling, what specifically leads you to respond to your teen in this way? Are you a parent who views your teen with a diagnosed disability with pity or as someone who can't do what is expected or can't help what is happening?

If you discovered that you are an enabler, don't get down on yourself. Instead, take steps to stop these patterns. In the next chapter, we will share some concepts and specific skills that you can use to become better able to empower your teen and increase the possibility of your teen becoming self-determined.

# Chapter 3
## Being the Copilot: A Coaching Approach to Parenting

After reading the last chapter, you might be wondering, "What are productive ways for parents to respond that wouldn't be considered enabling?" Or perhaps more productive ways of responding were obvious to you. Maybe you thought, "There's no way on earth I would respond like those parents did!" However, if the enabling responses seemed all too familiar, don't worry, because in this chapter you will learn skills to help you shift your approach from enabling to *empowering* so your teenager will become more independent.

## Empowering Your Teen

Empowering occurs when parents respond in ways that actively teach teens to take responsibility for their choices and to be accountable for their actions. Isn't that the goal for all parents: to help their children fully understand the powerful influence people can have on their own lives and to become confident at handling whatever shows up in life, especially when parents aren't around?

As you work through this chapter, you'll read examples and learn how to deliberately select coaching attitudes and responses that are designed to allow teens with attention-deficit/hyperactivity disorder (ADHD) or learning disability (LD) to become more self-determined. Here we borrow from the philosophy and skills used in the growing field of personal/life coaching to discuss a role that many parents already play when they stand on the sidelines encouraging, structuring, questioning, sharing suggestions, and holding teens accountable for following through. We call this more collaborative and empowering approach, a *coaching* approach to parenting. Now there will be times when parents still need to act as the absolute authority with their teens, setting clear rules and giving or allowing consequences when the issues are not conducive to collaboration. But in many of the day-to-day activities that your teen must master before taking off to college, we believe this more collaborative, coaching approach has great potential for getting your teen prepared.

Just as sports coaches partner with talented athletes to help them develop their skills and achieve success, life coaches partner with people to assist them in living the life of their dreams, one that is more fulfilling and balanced. This new helping profession provides a model that we believe can be a perfect middle ground between the important role parents need to play as the authority figure in their teenager's life and eventually letting go when their sons and daughters are mature, young adults.

## Learning New Ways to Communicate as a Coach

Coaching is a specialized relationship that involves a unique way of communicating. The purpose of a coaching relationship is to help people find their own answers to the challenges they face in life and identify what they want to change and make plans to make these changes happen. Through a coaching relationship, people are empowered to see the possibilities that exist in their lives and to make deliberate choices. Coaches are trained to have certain important attitudes and beliefs and to use some very specific skills. In the following pages, we have isolated some key coaching attitudes and skills that we think parents and teachers can apply in their daily interactions with teens.

**A coach needs to be nonjudgmental, compassionate, curious, and truthful.** The coach is not listening as a know-it-all or expert, trying to think of all the answers even before the entire situation is discussed. Instead, the coach listens in a caring manner and with curiosity about what is being said. In addition, the coach commits to being truthful in a loving way when the person isn't moving in the direction of his or her goals and dreams. Telling the "hard truth" allows the person being coached to see and face this truth.

**The coach stays on the sidelines and recognizes that the teen is truly in charge.** Think about it. Athletic coaches stay on the sidelines cheering, teaching, and playing an essential role before and after the big game, but they aren't in the game. The life coach fights any temptation to fix things for the client and to step over the sidelines by getting too involved or attached to the outcome.

**The coach exudes faith that the person being coached "has what it takes" to handle any struggle or challenging situation.** The person is not viewed as broken, weak, or dependent, but truly able to achieve her goals and dreams. The coach believes this all the time, especially when the person shrinks from new or uncomfortable situations and challenges. In fact, the coach does not worry or try to avoid failures but sees these situations as the times when the person can grow the most.

**Coaching is a collaborative partnership.** For the coaching relationship to work, there must be a collaborative partnership with both parties participating equally, even if they have different roles. The partnership is formed solely to help the person being coached to reach his goals, not goals the coach feels need to be addressed.

**The coach listens carefully to the message and the feelings behind the message.** Coaches must listen and help the person being coached to flush out what she is thinking, feeling, and wanting to create during the coaching sessions. Unlike in teaching, tutoring, or consulting, the coach is not acting as the expert giving answers. Instead, the coach is listening and allowing the other person to figure out what is going on now, what he wants to be different, and how to make the necessary changes.

**The coach asks open-ended questions that promote discovery.** As we said earlier, the coach listens with curiosity and asks powerful questions that lead the person being coached to greater discoveries. In fact, a highly skilled coach has no answer in mind, nor does she try to figure out the answer to the questions being asked. She is following the other person's words and clues and probing deeper and deeper to help that person get to the heart of the matter being discussed. Instead, coaches share suggestions, observations, and intuitive thoughts, knowing that the person being coached will ultimately decide whether to take them or leave them.

**Through listening and questioning, the coach helps the other person develop a more specific action plan.** Several skills, including goal-setting, planning, making commitments, and following through, are key to helping the person being coached in the development of the action plan needed to make the changes he wants. The coach helps the other person define exactly what steps will be taken as well as how and when to make change happen. In addition, the coach helps design a system for evaluating and accounting for the follow through on these commitments. (Learn more about developing an action plan in Chapter 5.)

# Example of a Coaching Conversation

What follows is an example of a coaching conversation between Kathy, the teen introduced in the previous chapter who perpetually oversleeps, and her dad.

## Beginning a Coaching Conversation

The first phase of the coaching dialogue puts the need for Kathy to change out in the open.

**Dad:** Kathy, our hassles this week made me realize that our mornings have to change. Because I won't be going to college with you, we need to talk about how to make mornings run smoother. I don't think it will be easy for you to wake up on your own at college if I continue to wake you up every morning. How do these morning hassles make you feel, and what do you think will happen when you have to wake yourself up at college?

**Kathy:** I hate starting the day with us yelling at each other. It makes the ride to school and my mornings just awful. I end up not listening in my first two classes because I'm sleepy and upset. I really never thought about how my trouble getting up in the morning might affect me when I am in college, but I can see now that it could be a problem.

## Envisioning a Better Way

This next phase of the coaching conversation lets Kathy dream about a better way.

**Dad:** Kathy, I used to sleep through alarms, too, but I know you can learn how to do this yourself if we make a plan and begin practicing now. Are you ready to change the way things are? If you could change our mornings, how would you like them to go?

**Kathy:** (Thinks for a while) Yes, I want to change. Well, I would really like to wake up on my own and meet you downstairs for breakfast, like my friends all do, but I am really not sure I can do that. I sleep through every alarm we buy. I would have to get my work done earlier, so I am not staying up so late and feeling so tired in the morning.

**Dad:** What would it take to make your dream happen? (Notices that Kathy gets quiet and tense, so he acknowledges her reaction) I can understand that change is scary. What's going on right now?

**Kathy:** I am worried that I'll sleep in, miss a lot of school, and flunk my classes. I'm worried that I can't learn how to do this by myself. Dad, how could you just stop helping me! And how would I get to school if you are gone?

**Dad:** I am sure this seems mean. I am still helping you but in a different way. I now realize how important it is that you learn these skills before you go off to college. And know that we will talk about what your Plan B will be if you miss driving in with me. But I believe we will find a plan so that you'll be sitting beside me, munching your bagel on the way to school.

## Moving to Action

In the final part of the coaching conversation, Kathy's father helps her to begin developing an action plan.

**Dad:** So, Kathy, what will it take for you to be ready and in my car by 7:30 starting this Monday? What steps can you take to make this happen?

**Kathy:** (Feeling insecure) I have no idea!!

**Dad:** I realize this kind of thinking is new for you. I'm curious, you woke yourself up when you went to camp last year. How did you do it?

**Kathy:** (Hesitantly begins to respond) Well, since you weren't there and I didn't have any school work, it was easier. I set two alarms, one near my bed and one across the room. I set the loudest one across the room to go off first. When I got out of bed, it was cold, and by walking across the room, I began to wake up. I had trouble being late the first couple of mornings because I fell back into a deep sleep. I then set the second alarm to go off two times. But I'll need more than loud alarms; I'll also need to figure out how to get my work done earlier.

**Dad:** I just want you to know that I believe in you, and I know that you can learn how to do this. You can talk with your friends to get ideas and then we can talk again tomorrow with your mother. We'll work together so you can learn how to wake yourself up now before it really causes you problems at college.

## Analyze the Example

After reading about Kathy and her dad, give yourself a minute to analyze the conversation and Kathy's dad's approach. How were coaching attitudes and skills applied in this conversation?

**The coach needs to be open, nonjudgmental, curious, and truthful.** Kathy's father's words are not judgments, labels, or put-downs like "You drive me crazy" or" You are so stubborn!" And he honestly shares his point of view and makes sure that his feelings don't get in the way. He's not defensive when his daughter expresses strong reactions to his questions and the realization that he means business. He doesn't minimize her feelings.

**The coach stays on the sidelines and recognizes the person is truly in charge.** Kathy's father focuses the discussion on her, prompting her to think about how the current patterns impact her now and in the future. He also recognizes that Kathy has to select a plan of action that she believes in and one that will work for her.

**The coach recognizes that the person is strong and capable and that failures and challenges are valued opportunities for growth.** The fact that Kathy's father decided that he will no longer fix her morning problems shows that he values her need to struggle. Kathy's father doesn't "cave" when she expresses her fears; instead he expresses faith in her even when she has doubts.

**Coaching is a partnership.** While Kathy's father makes it clear that he won't play the same old morning games, his tone and approach set the stage for a partnership in which Kathy's involvement and input are valued. His openness to Kathy's honest reactions sets the stage for their partnership. He enlists her commitment to collaborating and reinforces that he is still available to help her in a different way.

**The coach asks open-ended questions that promote discovery.** Kathy's father ends the first part of the conversation with open-ended questions that allow Kathy to reflect on the need for change. He also asks open-ended questions about her reactions to the thought of change. In moving Kathy to action, he asks questions to encourage her to think about what might help her get up on time by reflecting on a situation when she did wake up successfully on her own.

**The coach listens carefully to the message and the feelings behind the message.** Kathy's dad isn't just "hearing" her words but he also notices her feelings. Her facial reactions let him know that she was having strong feelings and he encouraged her to share them.

If you want some more practice with using coaching attitudes and skills, review the worksheet at the end of this chapter. It lists the other scenarios from Chapter 2 along with the original enabling response and has a column for you to fill in possible coaching responses and a column for you to identify the attitudes and skills you used. Also included is a worksheet to help you prepare for your conversation.

## Applying Coaching Attitudes and Skills

After reading this chapter, it's time to combine what you have learned in the last chapter with the coaching information in this new chapter. By using the coaching attitudes and skills outlined in this chapter, you too can begin to prepare your teen for the day when he goes off to college. Think about how you might have a coaching conversation with your teen. Remember to use the following steps.

1. Select a reoccurring situation that you face with your son or daughter and think how you could respond by using a coaching approach. Better yet, involve your teen in selecting an ongoing problem that she wants to change. Let your teen know that you are trying out some new skills from this book!

2. Write down the questions and responses you might try during each phase of a coaching conversation. How do you plan to apply coaching attitudes and skills throughout this conversation? Reread each of the coaching attitudes and skills. Which ones do you see yourself applying? Which have you not included in your plan? Which will be hardest for you to apply and why? Who can you ask to support you in your efforts to apply coaching to your parenting?

3. Now try out the first phase of your coaching conversation. Then the second, then the third. Keep a diary and jot down what you said and how your teen reacted. What went well? What didn't work? Why not? Be curious about what went wrong. Ask your teen for feedback. Having another adult to talk with as you try out a coaching approach might also be helpful.

4. Consider whether you may need to involve a third party to coach your teen. Is there another family member, neighbor, older college-age cousin, or mentor who might

be more able to play this coaching role with your teen? Do you and your teen need counseling or therapy to deal with some of the blocks to communication? What about finding a life coach in your community or using one of the organizations we have listed in the resource section of this guide to find one? Certainly, you can still apply these skills in daily life with your teen and do what you can to become part of the solution!

5. Check out all the coaching resources in the resource section of this book. You might even want to take a course, read more, or sign up for a webinar!

Now that you have some new attitudes and skills to help you take a coaching approach to parenting your teen, let's look at ways to evaluate your teen's readiness for college.

# More Practice Using a Coaching Approach to Parenting

| Teen and the Situation | An Enabling Response | Impact of Enabling Response |
|---|---|---|
| Tom forgot about science poster due tomorrow. | Tom's mother drops what she is doing and takes him to the store and stays up late helping him. | Tom learns his mom will bail him out and he misses the chance to learn about what he could do to prevent this type of problem. |
| Heather has many missing assignments. | Heather's mom calls the school and demands a meeting to make sure that the teachers communicate so Heather won't miss any assignments. | The environment changes to make sure Heather does her work. Heather doesn't learn to handle her assignments on her own, a skill she will need in college. |
| Christopher isn't packing his lunch, preparing his breakfast, or doing his laundry. | Christopher's mom sets the new expectations, but then takes over when he doesn't take charge. | Christopher doesn't have an opportunity to learn how to fit these important daily living skills into his day and week, skills he will need to learn soon. |
| Ella has several papers due at the same time and has procrastinated at starting them. | Ella's mom calls the teachers and asks for extensions as indicated on her IEP. | Ella doesn't learn how to plan ahead to prevent tough weeks when there are several big assignments due, something that will occur in college |

| **A Coaching Approach:** Fill in a possible coaching approach that could be used. | **Coaching Attitudes Used:** Reread the chapter and identify the coaching attitudes and skills. |
| --- | --- |
| | |
| | |
| | |
| | |

# Holding a Coaching Conversation Worksheet

1. **Beginning a Coaching Conversation**

   Questions I would ask:


   How my teen might react?


   Reread the coaching attitudes and skills and select responses
   that might be more "coaching like."


2. **Envisioning a New Way**

   Questions I would ask:


   How my teen might react?


   Reread the coaching attitudes and skills and select responses
   that might be more "coaching like."


3. **Moving to Action**

   Questions I would ask:


   How my teen might react?


   Reread the coaching attitudes and skills and select responses
   that might be more "coaching like."

# Chapter 4
## Is Your Teen Ready for Take-Off?

As we have said, getting into college is only half the battle. By now you are aware of the many other issues and challenges that await your teen at college, but how will you know if your teen is ready for this life experience? What information do you both need to make important decisions? How will you get a clear picture of the skills your teen has acquired that will make the college adjustment go smoothly and, conversely, the skills that really need to be developed so that your teen doesn't experience too much turbulence when it's time to take off and fly solo? Certainly, you and your teen can use the question "Are you ready for take-off?" to reflect and discuss how ready she is. You can begin to sort out the many factors needed to answer this question through the open-ended conversations you will have as you try on a coaching approach. But, having this conversation isn't that easy for many parents and teens.

In this chapter, we provide you with some tips and a tool to start looking more carefully at your teen's readiness by zooming in on the behaviors that will become the focus of your coaching conversations. The College Readiness Surveys at the end of this chapter are designed to help you and your teen talk and think about college readiness in an unemotional way. Taking the surveys is the first step in laying out a Personalized College Readiness Program that will allow you to coach your teen as he develops the skills needed to take over the controls. We've used these surveys in our work with teens and families and believe they will allow you and your teen to look at things more carefully and to talk openly about how life is going right now.

A note of caution should be introduced here, however. After reading this guide, you may be ready to dive in and talk about the surveys with your teen. However, you probably need to stop and think a bit more about how you are going to introduce the surveys and the topic of college readiness to your teen, since many teens, even those diagnosed with attention-deficit/hyperactivity (ADHD) or learning disability (LD), just assume that they will be successful at college. Because they may have good grades and haven't encountered many problems to date, they just can't understand what all the fuss is about. Also, they may not have the most astute self-understanding or ability to accurately observe themselves. Let's face it: It's impossible for them to have a precise view of what lies ahead, just around the corner in college. Having a conversation about developing "college readiness" with no warning might cause them to shut down and deny any need to do anything differently during the remaining time in high school. So, before actually introducing the College Readiness Surveys, it might be helpful to lay a little groundwork, so that your teen will be more open to using the time that remains during high school to get ready for college.

## Now Is the Time to Stretch and Grow

A healthy level of worry and anxiety can act as an important alarm, signaling the need to face some hard truths about college. Certainly, it is not the goal of this guide to frighten you or your teen! However, once you begin talking about college readiness, don't be surprised if you and your teenager feel some anxiety. We think that facing real feelings of anxiety and taking time to learn more about the differences between college and high school will help you both see the value in using the remaining time to prepare your teenager for college. Let your teenager know that you will work together to minimize future problems. Getting the facts can be enlightening and empowering if there is time to prepare. This guide can only be of help if you are both in agreement that now is the time to stretch and grow and get ready for what lies ahead, so be creative about what you can do to get your teen working with you.

Outlined below are several activities that you can work on with your teen that may help her begin to realize how different college is going to be from high school.

## Review the Admissions Criteria

One surefire way to wake up any teen and prod him to stretch and grow is to investigate what it will really take for him to be accepted into the college of his choice. Ask your teen to make a list of the top five to seven colleges he is dreaming of attending. Then have your teen visit the admissions websites of these colleges. Most websites will list the course requirements that entering first-year students must have to apply to the college. In addition, admissions websites frequently list a profile of the past year's entering freshman class. These profiles can give a clue about what the admissions committee uses for criteria for selecting applicants to that college. You'll want to know the following:

- What was the mean high school grade point average (GPA) of the entering freshman class?

- What were the mean SAT scores?

- How many Advanced Placement classes did they take?

- What types of outside and leadership activities did they pursue?

- What was the class ranking of the teens in last year's freshman class?

**Ready for Take-Off**

Check published catalogues (listed in our resources section) that you can buy or borrow from the library that may also have this type of information. Have your teen make a table of these facts. Then have a heart-to-heart talk about how or whether your teen is on track for being accepted to one of these colleges.

## Visit Colleges

We believe it is never too early for teens to visit a college campus and get a firsthand look at this new world. Unless teens have been to an actual college, they can't formulate a clear concept of what it is like. They don't understand that each department has its own building and that there is a different building for eating, living, and separate libraries. Just getting a feel for the size and the layout of a 2- or a 4-year college can help a teen get a better grasp of that world. If at all possible, visit the campus Disabilities Services Office and ask if any students with a diagnosis similar to your son's or daughter's diagnosis would be free to talk to both of you. A face-to-face discussion with a college student who has disabilities that are similar to your teen's can make a significant impression. Make sure you ask the college student some probing questions, such as: How ready was he for college? What were some of the struggles encountered during the transition? What did he wish he had known in high school before coming to college? What would he have done differently? What advice would he give to your teen and you about how to get ready? It is hoped your teen will come away inspired that attending college is a real possibility.

## Learn More About the Differences

Have your teen do a web search on the differences between high school and college or what it takes to be ready for college. This information can help her better understand what she might face during this life transition. For example, while writing this chapter, we did a search and got 12,000,000 hits when typing in "differences between high school and college." When we searched for "college readiness for teens with ADHD or LD," we got 10,700 hits. In addition, in searching YouTube with these same terms, we got over 100 hits. Of course, you have to pick and choose to find the best sites, but know that you can find great information and videos about college transition everywhere.

## (Picture-Perfect) Predictors of College Success

We hope, after these searches and visits, that your teen is now onboard and open to talking about college readiness. At this point, we're back to the question of how do you evaluate your teen's readiness. Researchers studying the factors that predict college success in nondisabled students have learned that good grades in high school and high standardized test scores may not be the only predictors of success in college (DeBerard, Spielmans, & Julka, 2004; Kuh, Kinzie, Schuh, Whitt, & Associates, 2005; Mattson, 2007; Pritchard & Wilson, 2003; Ridgell & Lounsbury, 2004). A number of psychological and emotional factors have been identified that also affect a student's eventual success in college. These factors include such qualities as

- possessing strong self-confidence;
- being achievement oriented;
- demonstrating persistence when faced with a challenge;
- setting a clear goal for attending college;
- maintaining good emotional health;
- forming positive social relationships;

- effectively coping with stress; and
- having good self-regulation skills.

These are all important factors that, in part, dictate whether students stay in school and graduate. Less is known about what factors predict success in college for students diagnosed with ADHD or LD, but we can say that these teens may have more problems than others in many of the psychological or emotional qualities listed above. So, besides looking at your teen's report card and standardized test scores, you and he need a way to systematically evaluate all the skills that might be needed to be ready for college.

## College Readiness Surveys

To help you with this evaluation process, we have provided two College Readiness Surveys at the end of this chapter, one for your teen and one for you, to make it easier for you to discuss your teen's readiness for college. These surveys inquire about many of the skills and qualities mentioned above that researchers consider important to success in college. We also checked with the real experts—college students with ADHD or LD—and included their input. The College Readiness Surveys will help you identify the goals that will be the focus of your coaching conversations in the weeks and months ahead.

No matter how much time remains before graduation from high school, know that you and your teen will be ahead of the game because you are thinking and talking about college readiness now. While we hope that parents of ninth and tenth graders are reading this guide, we also want parents of seniors who are about to go off to college to know that you still have time to start your training program.

Although we created the College Readiness Surveys initially as tools for working with families of high school students who wanted help getting ready for college, the surveys have also been used in local and national presentations as tools for parents, professionals, and teens in developing a strategic training plan for college. We offer these for your use in designing your teen's Personalized College Readiness Program. To get started, just follow the steps below.

1. Use the following survey to rate your teen in each skill area needed for success in college. A survey has been provided for your teen as well. You and your teen will independently rate skill areas on a scale from 1 to 3, with 1 = *not true of me*, 2 = *somewhat true of me*, and 3 = *very true of me*.

2. Score the surveys by totaling up the ratings for each section and then dividing the score by the total possible score listed at the end of each of the sections, and then multiply by 100. This will provide a percentage score for that section of the survey. Just like in school, the higher scores might be interpreted positively, meaning your teen has mastered a number of skills on that section of the survey. Lower scores would suggest that your teen has not mastered most of the skills in that section of the survey.

3. Use the Skills Analysis Worksheet at the end of this chapter to summarize which sections of the survey should become the focus of your training program.

4. Compare the differences between your ratings and your teen's ratings. This could be interesting, to say the least. We would suggest that you each look at the other's ratings in private to avoid arguing about whose rating is right.

Instead, consider doing the following:

- Compare your ratings on the various sections of the survey and find where there is agreement.

- If there are major differences in your ratings, we suggest that you each write out your reasons for the ratings and then read each other's comments privately.

- Do your ratings change based on what you read?

- If you can't come to agreement or productively discuss vastly different ratings, then agree to calculate the averages for these items.

5. Compare which items you agreed were mastered (rated 3), are in progress (rated 2), or were not mastered (rated 1). Make a list of these areas of strength and weakness.

6. Use the Skills Analysis Worksheet to develop a timeline for your Personalized College Readiness Program.

7. Count the remaining months or weeks until your teen takes off to college. Count how many skills were rated 2 or less, and divide the remaining months or weeks by the number of skills. If your teen is 24 months away from going to college and has 24 skills rated under 2 (lucky you!), then you would need to work on one skill every month to complete your training plan. If your teen only has 15 weeks until she goes off to college and there are 15 skills rated under 2, then your training plan will need to move more quickly with one skill being worked on each week. This will give you both a rough estimate of how many skills you need to work on each week or month to increase the odds of your teen having a less bumpy

solo flight. Of course, the further your teen is from college, the more time she has to slowly develop each skill; the closer your teen is to college, the more intensive your training process will need to be. Know that you can still work on skills during the first year of college, if your teen is cooperative.

In the following chapters we will share more specific information to help you develop and implement your teen's Personalized College Readiness Program for the skills your teen needs to develop. In Chapter 5 you will get more specific guidance on how to set goals and gradually move out of the pilot's seat, become the copilot, and eventually leave the cockpit altogether. Then there are chapters that provide tips, resources, and coaching reminders for each section of the College Readiness Surveys. Chapter 6 provides ideas for promoting the self-determination skills necessary for "goal-directed, self-regulated, autonomous behavior" (Field et al., 1998), including many of the skills we've listed on the survey in the areas of self-knowledge, self-advocacy, and self-management. Chapter 7 shares ideas to help teens develop the essential daily living skills, those nonacademic skills that your teen must have to survive on his own. Chapter 8 provides tips to consider if your teen has identified weakness in any of the essential academic and study skills that learning in college will demand. These three chapters are designed to be used as references where you can flip through the pages and find some great ideas and resources as you collaborate on your teen's training program.

So, now it's time to take the surveys . . .

# The College Readiness Survey for Teens:
## Are You Ready?

So you are excited about going to college and the idea of being on your own, right? But how ready are you really to successfully manage life on your own? Getting accepted at the college of your choice is only half the battle. Success takes more than strong academic skills. Just ask a friend or relative who is in college, and they will tell you about all the decisions you will have to make and the new challenges you will face. But don't get worried. Take action now instead! This survey can be used for you to rate yourself in each skill area needed for success in college. Be daring and ask your parents and teachers to rate you too! Your percentage in each category will give you an idea of how you are currently doing in each skill area.

Rate each of the following items on a scale from 1 to 3, with 1 = *not true of me*, 2 = *somewhat true of me*, and 3 = *very true of me*. For any items rated 1 or 2, make a plan to improve in these areas before going to college. Set one or two goals for each grading period throughout the year and then retake the survey to chart progress and select new goals.

## SELF-DETERMINATION

### I. Self-knowledge

I know a lot about myself and am aware of

_____ My talents, interests and my dreams for the future.

_____ My feelings and reactions when I have to get used to new people, places, and situations and what helps me adjust.

_____ My strengths and weaknesses in my academic and learning skills.

**Your self-knowledge score: _____ /9 × 100 = _____%**

## II. Self-Advocacy/Communication Skills

I can

____ Easily introduce myself to new people and hold conversations with others.

____ Clearly express my strengths and weaknesses to my teachers or other people.

____ Admit when I don't understand something in class and comfortably ask for help.

____ Easily find the help or support I need when I have a problem.

____ Express my thoughts well, even when I have a different view or opinion, and stand firm when needed.

____ Talk with the other people involved in any conflict and problem-solve to handle the situation.

**Your self-advocacy/communication score: ____ /18 × 100 =____%**

## III. Self-management

I can

____ Listen and understand what my friends and family members are saying about me without getting defensive.

____ Regularly set realistic goals for myself in all areas of my life.

____ Develop a plan to reach my goals and can put it into action.

____ Periodically think about my progress in reaching my goals and make modifications as needed.

____ Persistently deal with any challenge without becoming frustrated until I find an acceptable solution.

____ Observe my emotions and deal with them productively.

**Your self-management score: ____/18 × 100 = ____%**

# DAILY LIVING SKILLS

## I. Self-Care

I can

____ Wash and care for my own clothes.

____ Take any medications I need with few or no reminders.

____ Make my own doctor appointments and call to refill my prescription medications.

____ Prepare meals or choose healthy foods for my daily meals.

____ Get adequate exercise to remain healthy.

____ Manage money well and be trusted with credit cards.

____ Make good decisions about how to handle stress.

**Your self-care score: ___/21 × 100 = ____%**

## II. Organization

I can

____ Organize my room and possessions with few or no reminders.

____ Keep track of my important possessions and find them when I need them.

**Your organization score: ____/6 × 100 = ____%**

## III. Time Management

I can

____ Awaken myself each day and get out the door without much help from my parents.

____ Send myself to bed each night at a reasonable time.

____ Make good decisions about know how to balance fun, chores, and schoolwork.

____ Get places on time with no problem.

**Your time-management score:** ____/12 × 100 = ____%

**Your total Daily Living Skills score:** ____/39 × 100 = ____%

## <u>ACADEMIC SKILLS</u>

### I. Self-Knowledge

I know

____ My learning style and can find ways to help me learn and study best in different classes.

____ When and where I need to study to get the best results.

____ How to motivate myself to face difficult assignments.

**Your self-knowledge score:** ____/9 × 100 = ____%

### II. Study Skills

I know how to

____ Take notes from my reading assignments.

____ Take complete notes in class that are useful to me when I study for exams.

____ Identify what is important when I am reading.

____ Organize my ideas and write and edit my own papers.

____ Prepare for tests and final exams.

____ Review my class notes, assigned readings, and other materials on a regular basis.

____ Use the help available in school when I don't understand something or want to improve how I study.

**Your study skills score:** ____/21 × 100 = ____%

### III. Time Management

I can

_____ Set up my own study schedule.

_____ Consistently complete daily assigned homework.

_____ Develop a system for keeping track of due dates for all of my assignments.

_____ Stay on top of my reading assignments.

_____ Write assigned papers, study for tests, and complete long-term projects in a timely manner.

**Your time management score: _____/15 × 100 = _____%**

**Your total Academic Skills score: _____/45× 100 = _____%**

Now total the number of skills rated 2 or less: TOTAL = _____

You will use this score on the Skills Analysis Worksheet found on p. 68.

# The College Readiness Survey for Parents: How Ready Is Your Teen?

Will your teen be successful in college, or will your teen be one of the students who doesn't return for a second year or does not graduate? This survey was created from interviews with college students and what is known about what it takes to be successful in college. Think about your teen as you rate each item on a scale from 1 to 3, with 1 = My teen hardly ever does this, 2 = My teen does this sometimes, and 3 = My teen does this most of the time. Have your teen complete the teen's version of this survey as well. Have a conversation about what areas are strengths and what areas are weaknesses, and make a plan to improve any areas you both rated as a 1 or a 2. Set one or two goals for each grading period throughout the year, and then retake the survey to chart progress and select new goals.

## SELF-DETERMINATION SKILLS

### I. Self-Knowledge

My teen knows and is aware of his/her

_____ Talents, interests, and dreams for the future.

_____ Feelings and reactions when adjusting to new people, places, and situations and what helps during the adjustment process.

_____ Strengths and weaknesses in academic and learning skills.

**Self-knowledge score: _____/9 × 100 = _____%**

### II. Self-Advocacy

My teen can

_____ Easily introduce himself/herself to new people and hold conversations with others.

_____ Clearly express his/her strengths and weaknesses to teachers or other people.

_____ Admit when he/she doesn't understand something in class and comfortably ask for help.

_____ Easily find the help or support he/she needs when any problem arises.

_____ Express his/her thoughts well, even when he/she has a different view or opinion, and stand firm when needed.

_____ Talk with the other people involved when there is a conflict and problem solve to resolve the situation.

**Self-advocacy score: _____/18 x 100 = _____%**

### III. Self-Management

My teen can

_____ Listen and understand what his/her friends and family members are saying about him/her without becoming defensive.

_____ Regularly set realistic goals in all areas of life.

_____ Develop a plan to reach his/her goals and put them into action.

_____ Periodically think about his/her progress in reaching these goals and makes modifications as needed.

_____ Persistently deal with any challenge without becoming frustrated until he/she finds an acceptable solution.

_____ Observe his/her emotions and deal with them productively.

**Self-management score: _____/18 x 100 = _____%**

**Your total Self-Determination Skills score: _____/45 x 100 = _____ %**

# DAILY LIVING SKILLS

## I. Self-Care

My teen can

____ Wash and care for his/her own clothes.

____ Take any medication he/she needs with few or no reminders.

____ Make his/her own doctor appointments and call to refill prescription medications.

____ Prepare meals or choose healthy foods for daily meals.

____ Get adequate exercise to remain healthy.

____ Manage money well and be trusted with credit cards.

____ Use acceptable strategies to manage stress.

**Self-care score: ____/21 × 100 = ____%**

## II. Organization

My teen can

____ Organize his/her room and possessions with few or no reminders.

____ Keep track of his/her important possessions and find them when needed.

**Organization score: ____/6 × 100 = ____%**

## III. Time Management

My teen can

____ Awaken himself/herself each day and get out the door without any help from me.

_____ Send himself/herself to bed each night at a reasonable time without any reminders from me.

_____ Make good decisions and know how to balance his/her time between fun, chores, and schoolwork.

_____ Get places on time with no problem.

**Time-management score: _____/12 × 100 = _____%**

**Your total Daily Living Skills score: _____/39 × 100 = _____%**

## ACADEMIC SKILLS

### I. Self-Knowledge

My teen knows

_____ His/her learning style and can find ways to help himself/herself learn and study best in different classes.

_____ When and where he/she needs to study for the best results.

_____ How to get motivated to face difficult assignments.

**Self-knowledge score: _____/9 × 100 = _____%**

### II. Study Skills

My teen knows how to

_____ Take notes from reading assignments.

_____ Take complete notes in class that are useful when he/she studies for exams.

_____ Identify what's important when he/she is reading.

_____ Organize his/her ideas and write and edit his/her papers.

_____ Prepare for tests and final exams.

_____ Review class notes, assigned reading, and other materials on a regular basis.

_____ Use the help available in school when he/she doesn't understand something or wants to improve how he/she studies.

**Study skills score:** _____/21 × 100 = _____%

## III. Time Management

My teen can

_____ Set up his/her own study schedule.

_____ Consistently complete daily assigned homework.

_____ Develop a system to keep track of due dates for all assignments.

_____ Stay on top of his/her reading assignments and has ways to comprehend what he/she reads.

_____ Write assigned papers, prepare for tests, and complete long-term projects in a timely manner.

**Time-management score:** _____/15 × 100 = _____%

**Your total Academic Skills score:** _____/45 × 100 = _____%

Now total the number of skills rated 2 or less: TOTAL = _____

You will use this score on the Skills Analysis Worksheet on the following page.

# Skills Analysis Worksheet
## Analyzing Your Survey Answers

1.  Which skill area displays strengths (rated highest)? Add up the numbers and circle one of the skill areas listed below that corresponds to the highest score.

    **Self-determination Skills:**
    • Self-knowledge  • Self-advocacy
    • Self-management:

    **Daily Living Skills:**
    • Self-care  • Organization
    • Time-management

    **Academic Skills:**
    • Self-knowledge  • Study skills
    • Time-management

2.  Which skill area needs to improve the most? Add up the numbers and circle one that corresponds to the lowest score.

    **Self-determination Skills:**
    • Self-knowledge  • Self-advocacy
    • Self-management:

    **Daily Living Skills:**
    • Self-care  • Organization
    • Time-management

    **Academic Skills:**
    • Self-knowledge  • Study skills
    • Time-management

3.  Go back and look at the areas that you and your teen agreed were rated below 3.

    How many of the skills did you rate 2 or lower? ____ Total

4.  Now count how many weeks until college begins? # _____ weeks. Divide this number by the total number of skills rated 2 or lower. This will give an estimate of how many weeks remain to work on each skill before college begins.

**Total skills rated 2 or lower ____ / ____ number of weeks until college**

# Chapter 5
## Designing Your Teen's Personalized College Readiness Program

Unfortunately, no flight schools exist to train your teen for his first solo flight, that is, life in college. Instead, we wrote this guide so that you can design a Personalized College Readiness Program with your teen. During the remaining time in high school, you and your teen will be able to hold regular coaching discussions to draw up very specific action plans targeted to your teen's unmastered skills discovered by taking the College Readiness Surveys in the previous chapter. For your readiness program to be successful, you will need to apply all of your new coaching attitudes and skills to gradually move out of the pilot's seat and eventually out of the plane.

In this chapter, we encourage you to think of ways to hand over the controls to your teen as you let go of the role you have been playing. We present specific steps on how to get started, set clear and realistic goals, jointly develop step-by-step action plans, and create ways to evaluate and modify those plans.

### Handing Over the Controls

As you make progress on developing your Personalized College Readiness Program, we encourage you to keep in mind ways to deliberately hand over the controls to your teen or to evaluate whether it's time to move yourself out of the "cockpit" altogether. In addition, you will always need to be thinking about your bottom line. In other words, what is it that you will no longer be willing to do for your teen? You will also need to decide on the consequences that you are willing to allow your teen to experience as she learns how to fly solo. We understand that watching your teen struggle as she learns to do things on her own may be one of the greatest challenges you will face. However, we want to remind you that you really are an expert at doing this. You've done it hundreds of time throughout your teen's life, whether it was when she learned to take a shower, play outside, ride a bike, cook breakfast, or drive a car on her own. In each of these instances you taught her some rules or strategies, collected information to see if she "got it," and, eventually, you let go. And yes, there have been scraped knees, some big mistakes, lots of lessons, and it's likely you've had your share of challenging emotions along the way. But you really are already an expert at handing over the controls to your son or daughter!

In most cases during your teen's Personalized College Readiness Program, you will choose to gradually hand over the controls. This approach allows your teen to slowly learn to do all the remembering, thinking, and planning that you have been doing, as you gradually decrease your involvement. Yet, there may be rare situations when you decide to pull away abruptly or go "cold turkey." You may choose this path for several reasons. Sometimes, there just may not be enough time before your teen goes to college. We also realize that, at times, teens may not be taking responsibility for a skill, not because they can't but because it seems too hard. Or they don't want to grow up. Or they'd rather have you do it for them. Occasionally, teens may not have experienced the consequences of their behavior and don't see the need for change. In these instances, simulating the world of college and letting your teen see what happens without you might be a wise idea. Since he is still living at home, you will be able to help him fix things if he encounters any difficulty.

Letting go and decreasing your involvement with any of the skills on the College Readiness Survey in Chapter 4 will follow much the same pattern that you followed in the past, with one big difference: Now your teenager is capable of collaborating with you in the design of actual plans. So, let's get started!

## Personalized College Readiness Program

Giving your son or daughter choices and forming a collaborative coaching relationship are critical to the success of the program you design and the coaching discussion you have. People, and that includes teens, are more motivated to change when they have a say in the change being expected. So, before you get started, put on your coaching hat and take off your directive, "total authority" hat. It's best to begin the new partnership with your teen by fighting the urge to take charge. Keep in mind that you are now using a coaching approach to parenting as you read the following steps for designing your teen's Personalized College Readiness Program. We have also provided a worksheet to facilitate this process on page 89 at the end of this chapter.

### Step 1: Deciding On a Time for Your Coaching Discussions

You and your teen will need to agree on a regular time when you will both be available to hold your coaching discussions. Having a special time set aside will ensure that this program doesn't get lost in the busyness of family life. We suggest that you consider setting aside time on the same day each week, if possible, and consider meeting weekly or at least twice a month. Of course, how often you meet will depend on how much time you have before starting college. Begin by asking your teen the following questions:

- How do you think we should move forward now that we have analyzed our responses to the College Readiness Surveys?

- When do you think would be a good time for us to begin working on the readiness skills we identified that need some work?

> **➥ Coaching Reminder!** This is the time to model coming to an agreement and demonstrating that you value your teenager's input. Be ready with some suggestions, but try not to dictate. The atmosphere that you want to create is one that is conducive to a creative collaborative discussion about this important project. Be open to new ideas! For example, one family we met agreed to do their first planning "discussion" through instant messaging. This was the teen's favorite mode of communication but was not as familiar for the parents. However, the parents soon discovered that the online chatting allowed them to be less emotional and wordy. Their teen appreciated that her input was valued and was then more agreeable to face-to-face discussions to iron out additional details.

## Step 2: Choosing the Skill(s) to Work On

Next, choose the skills that will become the focus of your coaching discussions. Truly, there is no right order, just what makes sense to the two of you. If you have ample time before college, you might agree to start with the skills that were somewhat mastered and rated as a 2 on the College Readiness Survey. Or, if your time is more limited, focusing initially on the skills that were rated as a 1 may be more critical. Or you might just go down the College Readiness Survey and work on your teen's unmastered skills in the order they show up on the survey. Whatever the case, make sure that you and your teen agree on which skill(s) you'll work on initially. You will return to this step periodically each time your teen's action plan produces positive results and it's time to decide what skill is next. The following are sample questions to consider using at this time:

- What skills would you like to focus on first?

- What is your opinion about where we should start?

## Step 3: Defining Goal(s)

Setting clear, realistic goals for making a life change isn't as easy as you may think. Typically, people first need to think broadly about the behavior they want to change before they pin down a specific goal. They must also deal with feelings that may come up as they consider changing the old, nonproductive, yet familiar habits and begin to entertain some new possibilities. Eventually, they will create a very specific goal to which they commit their time and effort.

Going about this without a plan can be tricky. Try these steps to create a specific goal:

> **➥ Coaching Reminder!** Look back at the sample coaching discussions in Chapter 4 with Kathy and her father, to see how he moved from a very broad discussion to a more specific one. If you have been the pilot in your teen's life, know that you both may find a coaching approach difficult and unfamiliar at first. Don't hesitate to let your teen know that you are trying out the new skills you are learning about in this guide and that this type of thinking may be new for him as well.

1. Discuss what is going on right now with the skill that your teen wants to work on. Ask broad questions like "What do you see that is going on right now when you try to do (fill in with the skill)?" or "What happens now when you try to do (fill in the blank with the skill)?" Follow up with "What might be getting in the way?"

2. Think and talk about what you are doing when your teen is trying to do (fill in the blank with the skill) as well.

> **➥ Coaching Reminder!** Be on the lookout for any reactions you and your teen may have as you begin to dream of new possibilities. It is predictable that your teen (yes, and even you) may begin to have fears and doubts crop up as you consider letting go of old ways. Use your new coaching attitudes and skills to be open to whatever shows up and talk about them.

3. Help your teen envision a better way for how things could go. To do this, consider asking the following questions:

"If you could change things, how would you like things to be?" "What would you want to have happen instead of what is happening now?" "What would doing (skill) differently look like?"

4. Ask these same questions about your involvement with the skill you are discussing: "What would you wish I would do differently?" and "What role do you wish I would play?"

5. Summarize the new possibilities that you both have just envisioned.

6. Develop a goal. Talk with your teen about the process of setting goals and find out what she already knows about this skill. If she lacks information, you might share the information below about SMART goals or suggest that she conduct an Internet search on setting goals.

7. Jot down a goal statement for a college readiness skill on which you have chosen to work.

8. Write a goal related to your behavior for each skill as it is worked on as well. Real change is a two-way street: It is likely that you will both need to change your behaviors.

9. Once goal statements are written, polish and refine them using the SMART model described below.

10. Give feedback on each other's goals. To demonstrate openness, ask your teen for feedback on your goal first.

## Setting SMART Goals

Much is now understood about how our thoughts and words affect our behavior. If we have vague goals and plans, then our accomplishments may be just as vague, or our plans may remain fuzzy and fail to materialize. The more precise and specific we are about what we want to design in our lives, the more likely it will be that we will use our conscious thought and energy to deliberately choose what we want to happen. One catchy acronym used often in the workplace and in education for goal setting is the term SMART. Each letter represents an important criterion for a well-written goal (For more information about SMART goal statements, see the Rose, 2006, and Conzemius & O'Neill, 2001, references in the resources section at the back of this guide).

A SMART well-developed goal statement meets all the following conditions:

**S = Specific.** The more detail included in the goal, the better able the person will be to focus his efforts. Goals need to state very clearly what the person wants to accomplish.

**M = Measurable.** This ties in with the notion of being specific. A SMART goal statement is easy to measure to determine if progress is made and to establish when the goal has been accomplished.

**A = Agreed to.** There are several interpretations of the letter "A" in the acronym. One that we particularly like is that "A" equals "agreed to." This means that the person has committed to taking action and is not complying to make others happy.

**R = Realistic.** Well-defined goals allow us to believe that we can, with different attitudes and behaviors, take the steps to make change happen. If goals are too easy or too lofty, we may lack the motivation to take action.

**T = Timely or Time sensitive.** A clear goal statement narrows down the time frame for achieving what the person wants to do. So often, we never take action because we don't define when we will do something, thus condemning a goal to the "realm of good intentions." Instead of saying "Someday I will lose weight, quit smoking, clean the garage," and so on, SMART goals state a very specific time frame.

As you will discover, making a goal SMART will take some time and thought. Let's look at some examples in the following table of vague goals versus SMART goals and the differences between them.

## Vague Goals Versus SMART Goals

| Readiness Skills | Vague Goal | SMART Goal | Differences |
|---|---|---|---|
| Academic Skills: study skills | I will study harder this grading period. | I will study 30 minutes daily, 5 days a week for subjects where my grade is a B or lower. | The vague study goal can't be measured and the SMART goal is precise, realistic, and progress will be easy to evaluate. |
| Daily Living Skills: organization and time management | I will go to bed earlier. | I will be in bed each school night no later than 10:30. | In the vague goal, there could be debate about what earlier means, not in the specific SMART goal. |
| Self-Determination Skills: self-advocacy | I want to be more social. | I will go out with friends or to an event 5 times each month. | The SMART goal is very targeted and will be easy to measure. |

## Step 4: Deciding How to Hand Over the Controls

Decide on how you will hand over the control for this skill and what your bottom line is before designing an action plan. Are you gradually going to hand over the controls or if the situation warrants going cold turkey? Think about how you might implement the approach you are planning to follow. What is your bottom line? What is it that you will no longer be willing to do? What consequences are you willing to allow your teen to experience?

## Step 5: Designing Step-by-Step Action Plans

Equipped with a list of skills, a clear SMART goal, the approach you will use to hand over the controls, and your bottom line, it is time to help your teen get specific about an action plan to reach her goal.

In this important step you will be asking a series of open-ended questions, listening carefully and reflecting what you hear, and at times sharing some suggestions. When you and your teen have finished fully discussing this step, you will both know what she is going to do, when she is going to do it, how you will both know if she did it, and a way to figure out how things are working. Of course, you should also be developing a step-by-step action plan for the changes you are making in your behavior in relation to your goals and be able to answer the same questions about your action plan.

1. Help your teen brainstorm some possible ideas for implementing his goal by asking questions similar to these: "What might help you reach this goal?" "What do you think would work for you?" "What has worked in similar situations in

➥ **Coaching Reminder!** Open-ended questions can encourage brainstorming to generate ideas. Tell your teen (and believe this yourself) that there is no right way or one rigid approach for performing the skill being discussed. What matters most is that your teen must believe in the ideas he generates. Remember, what you think will work is not really important here. Be prepared that your teen may act like Kathy did with her father and have "no idea." Just let there be silence so your teen can have time to think. This way of acting may be frustrating initially. Offer some suggestions with questions like "Is it is okay for me to share some suggestions?" and "Can I share some feedback and observations with you?" But remind yourself and your teen that these are only suggestions and not mandates. Avoid taking charge and telling your teen what to do or subtly pushing your ideas as the best ones. This is where the coaching attitudes and skills from the previous chapter will come into play. Remember, your main job as the coach or co-pilot is to pose questions. Review the attitudes and skills from Chapter 4 before joining your teen in a planning discussion.

the past?" "What do others do (ask friends, siblings) when they (fill in the blank with the readiness skill)?"

2. Share any observations of what you have noticed seems to work that your teen might adopt.

3. Encourage using the later chapters in this guide by looking

up the skill your teen is working on and reading those pages in the chapter to see if any of the tips and resources provided might be of use.

4. Help your teen decide which idea is best by restating the ideas you have heard in the previous step, or ask your teen, "So, what are some of the ideas you are coming up with to reach your goal?" "Which ideas do you think would work for you?" "Are you ready to decide on one idea? Which one is it?"

5. Help your teen make a step-by-step action plan that flushes out what she will do when, how she will remember to implement the changes she wants to make, what role she wants you to play, and a way to evaluate how things are going. You can do this by asking questions like "What steps will you take to do what you have decided?" "What do you need to do to put your new idea into place?" "What will help you remember to take these steps?" "What role, if any, would you like me or others to play in the plan?" "Do you want me to respond if the steps are or aren't taken? If so, how?" Ask for specific advice on what to do or say and what not to do or say.

6. Determine how you will keep track of progress by asking, "How will you keep track of progress?" "How will we know that you have done what you said you would?" "How will we know that you have mastered this skill?" "When and where will you and I talk to review progress and set new goals?" To flush out how to handle things at the progress check-in meeting, ask your teen, "How should that discussion be designed?" "What questions

should we ask about your plan?" "When your plan goes as you hoped, what should we do?" "When your plan doesn't go as hoped, what should we do?"

7. Write up what was discussed. Decide with your teen's input how to do this or offer to do this together before you end your coaching discussion. Having written goals and a plan will ensure that you are both on the same page.

➡ **Coaching Reminder!** Depending on what you decided about handing over the controls, be sure to evaluate if what your teen is requesting is a role that you think is okay. You can say "yes" if you agree and "no" if you don't, and make a counteroffer to your teen about the role he is asking you to play. If you are going cold turkey and abruptly removing yourself, restate why you are doing this and what you are willing to do and not do: Provide time to think of ideas, evaluate how things have gone, support, encourage, make suggestions, and so on.

## A Sample Coaching Discussion to Develop a Step-by-Step Action Plan

Using one of the situations we presented in Chapter 2, let's see what a coaching discussion that develops a step-by-step action plan could look like.

Remember Tom, the eleventh grader who has organizational problems and discovered late one night that he had forgotten to create a poster for his science class? Well, his mother did bail him out and drove him to Wal-Mart, knowing that this would be the last time she would do it. When Tom took the College Readiness Survey, he and his mother both agreed that he lacked the skills of keeping track of his assignments, and Tom heard from an older cousin how critical this skill is for eventual success in college. So he wanted to start his Personalized College Readiness Program by focusing on this skill area. Let's peek in on their first coaching discussion, in which Tom's mother has decided that she will start to hand over the control. They had set aside time on Saturday afternoon to have their discussion. We are joining them at Step 5 in the process, designing step-by-step action plans.

**Mom:** Tom, you have decided that you want to improve your ability to keep track of all of your long-term assignments (anything that isn't daily homework) with the goal of completing them at least 1 day in advance. What are some strategies you can use or some rules you can make for yourself that will allow you to reach this goal?

**Tom:** Well, I know a lot of my friends use the assignment book that our guidance counselors hand out, but this never worked for me. I forget to open it and look at it. I keep my daily homework in my notebooks and just open them when I sit down to do homework. That works for homework, but even when I write long-term assignments in my notebook, I don't remember them. I have no idea what would work.

**Mom:** Well, let's brainstorm some ideas. I'll go first. What do you think about putting reminders about your assignments in your phone or having your online calendar e-mail you reminders regularly so you won't forget?

**Tom:** No, I don't think that would work for me, I need a

bigger reminder, one I will see all the time. I might want to buy one of those big white boards. I could hang it in my bedroom and list all the big assignments for the next few weeks, including when they are due. Then, when I am done with homework, I could look up at the board and work on them a little at a time. I think that would work for me.

**Mom:** That sounds like a great idea! Do you want to keep thinking of ideas or do you think you have landed on a good one?

**Tom:** No, I think the white board would work.

**Mom:** Okay then, what steps do you need to take to get started with this plan?

**Tom:** Well, I need to buy a white board after school tomorrow and then go through all of my syllabi that are online and write down the big assignments, including the due dates for all my classes for the next month.

**Mom:** Sounds good! Do you think you need anything to help you remember to take these steps?

**Tom:** Yeah, I need to put them in my phone and set an alarm to go off before I leave school. How about I do that right now? (Puts task list in phone and sets alarm)

**Mom:** So what role would you like me to play in your plan? I know that sometimes I have nagged you a lot and made you mad, and then other times you wanted me to check with you and see what long-term assignments you had.

**Tom:** Because I have never done this by myself before, how about meeting when I get home tomorrow to go over my syllabi and make the list on my white board? Then, before I do homework, could you ask me what project I plan to work on each night?

**Mom:** This sounds good, and, at first, I am happy to do the planning with you and check on your progress. But how about if after 2 weeks, you do the white board on your own once a week and come and get me and show me the list, and then each night when you are ready to do homework you can come and tell me what project you plan to work on. That way you are learning to do this step without me being the reminder. Eventually, you'll need to do this without me, but, at first, you can use me to help you follow through. We will decide together when you feel you don't need me to check on any of the steps with you. How are you planning to keep track of the progress you are making at getting your long-term assignments done early, so you can reach your goal of finishing them completely 1 day before they are due?

**Tom:** I think I need to keep a list of all of my long-term assignments for the next couple of weeks on the white board with a column for the actual dates they are due and a column for the day I finish them. I can fill out the dates when I finish and we could see if I am really getting them done one day before they are due. Also, by having the list on the board, I will see what is left and how much time I have to do it.

**Mom:** That sounds like a great idea, the facts will be right there on the white board. When do you think you and I should sit down and review how things are going and where you are at reaching your goal? How will we know that it is time to work on a new skill from the College Readiness Survey?

**Tom:** I don't know. What do you think?

**Mom:** Do you have any ideas that make sense to you? (Note to parents: Even when pushed, Tom's mother is avoiding taking charge here.)

**Tom:** Hmmm . . . (silence for a few minutes). I really think we should talk once a week right now, maybe on the weekend, to see how I am doing and decide if I am making progress or not.

**Mom:** I agree that it will be obvious if you are getting long-term assignments done a day in advance or not. If we meet each week, we can decide if you still want me checking on you and if it is time to move to a new skill. I would suggest that when we see you getting all your long-term assignments done without me playing any role maybe for a 2-week period, we will know that it is time to move on to a new skill. What do you think?

**Tom:** Yeah, that makes sense to me.

**Mom:** What do you think about going to your computer right now and sending us both an e-mail summarizing the goal you are working on, the action plan we just made, my role in it, and our plan for evaluating your progress and for setting new goals?

**Tom:** Sure, no problem.

## When Things Aren't Going As Planned

We understand that along the way there will be setbacks, flare-ups, and emotions that are new to both you and your teen. However, our work with families has convinced us that if everyone is committed to preparing teens for college, then your coaching discussions to develop step-by-step action plans will go better with time and practice. It is also okay to acknowledge any tension you are feeling as you communicate about these issues or any old patterns that show up and block your ability to be the coach for your teen. In these circumstances, you might need to first deal with these communication patterns and emotional flare-ups by talking with your partner or even seeking help from a therapist or counselor.

If it becomes clear that you can't be the person having these coaching discussions with your teen right now, or maybe ever, then you might take a different approach. You might think about what other resource people you have in the family, neighborhood, school, or community who may be able to play a coaching role with your teen. Are there older teens in the family or neighborhood who might be willing to volunteer to be a mentor or coach for your college-bound teen who could join your discussions or even lead them? Is there anyone in the school or church who might be willing to use this book and lead a college readiness group?

Finally, know that there are professional coaches available who specialize in helping teens with attention-deficit/hyperactivity disorder (ADHD) or learning disability (LD) get ready for college. Although coaches are perfectly trained for this important role, sometimes they are not affordable because typically insurance does not cover these fees. However, there are organizations that offer coaching for high school and college students that you can contact and even some training programs that you can check out that might offer lower cost coaching. These are listed in our resource guide at the end of the book. Still, even if you can decide to use outside resources, you will always be the one talking with your teen on a daily basis. It is our hope that every parent and teen can still implement the coaching approach to parenting and follow some of the procedures outlined in this chapter to create new, more effective ways for teens with ADHD or LD to take the controls in important areas of their lives while they are still preparing for take-off.

## When the Program Is Working

Once you have had a series of successful coaching conversations, you and your teen will become familiar with moving through the five-step process in this chapter. During the remaining time your teen is in high school, you will have regular coaching discussions and follow these steps as you work on the skills from the College Readiness Surveys. We always want you to be creative and personalize your action plans to suit you and your teen. However, we also hope that you will both feel free to use the next three chapters, which are chock full of tips, resources, and some coaching reminders for the skills in each section of the College Readiness Surveys.

## Coaching Teens to Coach Themselves

As you both learn more about the coaching process, you will be able to use your new coaching attitudes and skills to hand over the controls to your teen even more frequently. You can do this by asking open-ended questions at any time, even in day-to-day life as your teen tells you about challenges she is facing and turns to you for advice. Even though these aren't scheduled coaching discussions, we hope you will use these occasions to help your teen practice figuring things out for herself. Instead of giving your opinion or providing direction, ask questions such as: "If you heard your friend tell you about a situation like this, what advice would you give or what questions would you ask yourself right now?" "What steps could you take to help you deal with this situation?" We really do hope that you will begin to apply a coaching approach to parenting in all of your interactions with your teen.

In addition, during the times that you are working on your teen's Personalized College Readiness Program, you can deliberately invite your teen to lead the coaching discussions or share this job with you. By doing so, you will give your teen practice coaching himself, which is the ultimate goal of all of your work together. To facilitate this process during your scheduled coaching discussions, ask questions such as: "How would you suggest that we proceed?" "What are the steps to follow as we talk about your Personalized College Readiness Program?" "How would you summarize what we are talking about and what questions should we think about?"

Asking open-ended questions like these will allow your teen to develop those important self-determination and executive functioning skills discussed throughout this book. It is definitely okay to encourage your teen to look over this chapter so she is aware of the steps that you are using during your coaching discussions. The more your teen understands and learns to use the five steps outlined in this chapter and learns to pose open-ended questions to herself, the more she will be able to take the controls and be ready for take-off!

# Designing Your Teen's Personalized College Readiness Program Worksheet

## HANDING OVER THE CONTROLS

1. What parenting patterns do you have that might block your ability to slowly hand over the controls or even to move out of the "cockpit" so your teen can practice flying solo while he is in high school?


2. What do you think you can do to prevent these patterns from stopping you from taking a coaching approach to parenting?


3. What worries do you have about meeting with your teen to begin working on your personalized training process? What will help you deal with these worries?


4. Who are the resource people in your family, neighborhood, church, school, or community that you can use to assist you in designing and implementing your teen's Personalized College Readiness Program?


5. Listed below are each of the steps you will follow in designing your teen's Personalized College Readiness Program. Make a list of some sample, open-ended questions you could ask that match your style. The one we have provided is just a guideline or a starting point. Try to come up with questions that will be more comfortable for you.

# Personalized College Readiness Program Planning Sheet

Use this form to organize and outline your readiness program. It may be helpful to create a separate form for each skill you and your teen choose to work on.

| | |
|---|---|
| **1. Discussions time(s)** | |
| **2. Skill(s) to work on** | |
| **3. Define goal(s)** | |
| **4. Determine approach and bottom line** | |

# Action Plan

| | |
|---|---|
| **1. Brainstorm ideas** | |
| **2. Decide on an idea** | |
| **3. Make an action plan** | • Steps to take<br><br>• Ways to remember<br><br>• Parent's role<br><br>• Track progress |
| **4. Evaluate action plan** | |

# Personalized College Readiness
## Program Planning Sheet

Use this form to organize and outline your readiness program. It may be helpful to create a separate form for each skill you and your teen chooses to work on.

| | |
|---|---|
| **1. Discussions time(s)** | Saturday at 11:00 |
| **2. Skill(s) to work on** | • Admit when she doesn't understand something in class and comfortably ask for help.<br><br>• Easily find the help or support he needs. |
| **3. Define goal(s)** | Pam: I will ask for help from someone at school at least once a week. |
| **4. Determine approach and bottom line** | Mom: I will no longer call or meet with school personnel on my own and will help my daughter figure out what help she needs, where to find it, and to practice asking on her own. |

# Action Plan

| | |
|---|---|
| **1. Brainstorm ideas** | Pam's ideas<br>When I am confused in class I can:<br><br>• Ask Ron or Sarah if they can answer my question instead of asking my mom.<br><br>• Email teacher since talking face-to-face is hard. |
| **2. Decide on an idea** | • I like the idea of emailing my teacher and asking my question this way, and if this doesn't work, I will come in early or stay after school to talk with my teacher. |
| **3. Make an action plan** | • Steps to take: During my morning and afternoon study hall, I will look over the work from that day and see if I am confused about anything.  Then I will write up an e-mail and let my mom look it over before I send it.<br><br>• Ways to remember:  I will put a post-it note in my assignment book that says:  "What confused you today?" And I'll move it each day when I look at my assignments during study hall.<br><br>• My mom's role: My mom will ask me if she doesn't get a draft e-mail from me that day asking my teacher for help. My mom agrees to read my e-mail and share any thoughts she has on what might need to be rewritten, but not tell me what to say. She will also have permission to ask me if I heard back from the teacher if I forget to tell her.<br><br>• Track progress: I will list every e-mail I send on my assignment calendar and a put a check mark when I hear back from the teacher. |
| **4. Evaluate action plan** | We will meet in 2 weeks to see how we are both doing with our goals. |

# Chapter 6
## Promoting Self-Determination Skills

For the past several decades, experts in the field of special education have grappled with the reason why some individuals with disabilities have more successful adult lives than others. This scrutiny led them to come to an understanding of the importance of self-determination (Field, Martin, Miller, Ward, & Wehmeyer, 1998; Wehmeyer & Field, 2007). A self-determined individual is aware of who he is, including his strengths and weaknesses. He can set his own goals and make plans to achieve these goals, which include finding help and appropriate resources when necessary. Most importantly, a self-determined individual can solve problems, make decisions, and regulate his own behavior. Success in college and in life requires self-determination skills so young adults can take the controls effectively and overcome any obstacles that stand in the way.

In this chapter, we share tips and coaching strategies for you to use in the development of action plans to improve your teen's skills in the area of self-determination, including self-knowledge, self-advocacy, and self-management. Based on the results of your teen's College Readiness Survey in Chapter 4, choose the skill you want to develop from those listed below and learn more about why this skill is important and how you can incorporate various activities and coaching questions into your action plan. Now, let's get to work developing your teen's self-determination by improving her self-knowledge, self-advocacy, and self-management skills.

# Skill: Self-Knowledge

Self-knowledge or self-awareness is achieved through a process that includes reflecting on ourselves and our experiences and discussing ourselves with others. Although there is no step-by-step guide to suddenly make a person more self-aware, we provide some strategies on increasing self-knowledge in this chapter, as well as share tips by the real experts—the parents and teens with whom we have worked.

## Determining Strengths and Hidden Talents

Once in college, young adults will be presented with opportunities, including selecting a major and ultimately a career path, that require self-knowledge of talents and interests, not just academic strengths. To make these decisions wisely, a teenager needs to know more about what he enjoys and is naturally inclined to do. Sometimes teens diagnosed with attention-deficit/hyperactivity disorder (ADHD) or learning disability (LD) become so narrowly focused on activities designed to improve their school performance (tutoring, counseling, coaching, etc.) that they neglect putting equal time into cultivating their unique talents, passions, and interests. To help your teen become more aware, ask her to consider the following tips.

**Keep a daily or weekly log.** List the activities selected during free time, rating them for interest and enjoyment. Sometimes, experiments in self-observation like this one can provide more insights than if parents share their observations.

**Review old report cards.** Talents, strengths, and interests can also show up as patterns in school. What comments did teachers make that point to talents and strengths? What talents might be hiding behind behaviors in the classroom that may have gotten him into trouble (e.g., doodling or drawing, singing, speaking out in class, etc.)?

**Experiment with new activities.** New activities, including joining an art or theatre class or the church youth choir or volunteering at a retirement home, might help her uncover a hidden talent or interest.

➡ **Coaching Reminder!** Ask your teen to think about the things he loved to do when younger and those that he continues to enjoy. Also, have him think about things he did that got him into trouble as these are often clues to activities that he is passionate about. For example, did he read books under the covers late into the night or hide them in boring school books in school? Does he doodle and draw all over his notebooks? Is he always helping neighbors do chores instead of doing chores around the house? Then think about what talents and interests might be hidden under these "misbehaviors."

You can also help to uncover hidden talents or interests by noticing when your teen is engaged in or talking about an enjoyable experience. This would be a perfect time to share that you notice that this activity has sparked a lot of emotion or passion and ask her if this might be a clue to a talent or interest.

## Reviewing Academic Strengths and Weaknesses

To assure a successful academic experience, you and your teen need to be clear about his academic and learning skills. Use the tips and questions below to build a more specific understanding of your teen's academic strengths, weaknesses, and the way in which her disability affects learning.

**Read over your teen's old report cards.** Pay specific attention to teacher comments. What positive comments were mentioned from year to year? What academic strengths might these comments match? What negative comments were noted, and what academic skills might be behind these more negative comments? Is it possible that your teen's disability was the reason for these negative comments?

**Look for patterns in your teen's grades.** In which classes does your teen do well and in which does he struggle? To identify weaknesses, talk about what your teen dislikes or has trouble doing. Talk about why these tasks might be hard. Ask your teen what subjects at school and tasks at home he avoids at all costs.

## Understanding and Accepting Disabilities

Does your teen really understand her disability and how it affects her? For example, does your teen make general statements like "I have an auditory processing problem" or "I have a nonverbal learning disability"? If you and your teen can't state specifically how this disability affects her at school, at home, and socially, then you both need to dig deeper. The following tips might help.

**Review the written report from previous evaluations.** Read these together and talk about what you are learning and make a list of any questions you have. This may include terms you don't understand or statements that you are both wondering about as you reread the report.

**Ask to meet with someone at your teen's school.** Perhaps you need a meeting with the special class teacher, the transition specialist, the psychologist who evaluated your teen, or the leader of the building-based intervention team who worked with your teen. Ask this person to help you both understand how your teen's disability shows up or affects your teen in school, at home, and socially. When you don't understand what is being said, be bold and ask for a clear explanation. Consider taping this meeting so you and your teen can listen to the explanation again.

➡ **Coaching Reminder!** Discuss your teen's diagnosis with him and whether you both really accept it. Do you think that either of you might be denying its existence by blaming others for problems that occur? Talk openly about the feelings you have, and ask your teen about his feelings about the label and having a disability. Acceptance of a disability or difference is similar to acceptance of a chronic illness. It is normal for you both to go through a variety of stages (denial, blame, anger, sadness) before coming to terms with the truth that something is different about how he learns. When you come to full acceptance, this may help your teen to do the same. Certainly, if you are in denial or blaming others or feeling guilty, angry, or sad, it is okay to let your teen know how you feel. Your honesty may encourage him to express his feelings.

**Talk with your teen about what the upside of having a disability might be.** Although this question may seem impossible to answer at first, give it careful thought. Have either of you seen any positives outcomes associated with your teen's disability? Seeing the blessings or gifts hidden in the struggles of having a learning or attention disability is a sign of acceptance. In fact, people who have studied successful adults with ADHD or LD have frequently pointed out that reframing or seeing the good in having a disability separates successful adults from those who are still struggling (Gerber, Reiff, & Ginsberg, 1996).

## Being Comfortable in New Places and Situations

Having a successful solo flight may depend on how well your teen adjusts to the new and unfamiliar setting at college as much as it does on her academic skills. Will she become homesick for family, friends, and high school? Or will she dive head first into all the freedom and opportunities of college life? Or will her adjustment period be somewhere in between these two extremes?

Whatever a teen's style of reacting to change, it is clear that going off to college is one of the most challenging adjustments teenagers will encounter. As we have said before, the familiarity of home and the consistent routine they have been used to for 13 years of school will be turned upside down. To facilitate a smoother transition, consider the following experiences.

**Try it out beforehand.** Find out if any of your local colleges have special transition programs for high school students to help them get ready for college. These "taste of college experiences" allow younger teens to live on a college campus for a week or longer in the summer. Students can see what dorm life is like, have a simulated college class, and be mentored by college students. If there are not transition programs in your area, consider having your teen take a class at a local college. Then you can both see how he adjusts to this new environment while still living at home.

**➡ Coaching Reminder!** To smooth the way and help your teen to adjust to college, it's important to first determine her typical response to change. Here are some questions to ponder that may help you and your teen clarify her style of reacting to changes. Ask her to:

1. Think back on the many transitions she has already experienced. Talk about how she adjusted to kindergarten, middle school, high school, camp, moving into a new house, going to a new church, joining a new club, and so on. What patterns do you both see as her typical response to these changes?

2. Look at more recent situations. What did she feel like at a party or school dance where there were unfamiliar people?

3. Think about what she did to help her adjust in a new situation.

4. Make predictions based on what you have learned about her previous patterns about how she might feel and react during the adjustment to college.

5. Consider strategies that might make the adjustment to college go smoother.

**Enroll in a bridge or transition program.** Once your teen is accepted to college, ask if summer "bridge" experiences are available. These experiences are typically for minority students, first-generation students, or students from smaller high schools. Find out if your teen can apply for this program. Even though these experiences will cut an entering freshman's summer short, they are invaluable in increasing a student's success in the first semester of college.

**Enroll in a summer session.** If the college your teen selects doesn't have a summer bridge program, create your own by having your teen attend the last session of summer school offered by the college. A formal or informal transition program will allow your teen to experience college in a quieter environment with fewer class demands. He will be able to familiarize himself with campus and dorm life. Be sure to submit your teen's documentation to the Disabilities Services Office as soon as he is accepted and before this summer session. That way, your teen can get the accommodations he needs while taking one or two classes in summer, when the campus is typically less frenetic. He will be ahead of the game by becoming familiar with the procedures for accessing resources on campus.

## Skill: Self-Advocacy

Many teens have told us they were blindsided by all the instant and differing ways they were expected to advocate for themselves at college. After unloading all your teen's possessions into his dorm room, as soon as you pull away, your teen will need to use his self-advocacy skills. He'll instantly be meeting new people and will be placed in new situations in which he will have to speak up as well as socialize. Just imagine: What will your teen do when there is a discussion about who gets which bed and desk in the dorm room? How will she handle going to the financial aid office to work out the terms of her student loan? What will your teen do when the Disabilities Services Office sends out an e-mail telling all newly cleared students to call or drop by to make an appointment to arrange accommodations? What about making phone calls to make appointments for meeting a local doctor to get a prescription, or going to campus health when he is sick? How will your teen talk with professors to arrange getting class notes or extended time for exams? Suddenly you are not around, and your teen has the entire job of meeting new people and advocating or speaking up for himself.

## Meeting New People

One of the top skills needed by any new college student is the ability to meet new people, start conversations, and keep them going. Once again, depending on your teen's unique temperament and disability, these skills might be a "no brainer" or might be overwhelmingly difficult for her to develop. Teens may have problems in this area as a result of either emotional or learning issues. More introverted teens may find it difficult to enter a room or go to an event where they don't know anyone else and initiate a conversation, even if they know how to have a conversation. Some of the young adults we meet have even more serious social anxiety issues that totally shut them down and keep them out of the social scene of college altogether.

Teens with nonverbal learning disabilities often lack the ability to interpret the subtleties of social interaction and may steer away for social situations or even act inappropriately in these settings. Teens with a language-based learning disability may have trouble in social situations for different reasons. Their slower cognitive style may make it harder for them to organize their thoughts into words or find the right words to express themselves. These teens complain that they find the give-and-take of conversation to be very painful as they take longer to interpret what others say and have to pause for a longer time to respond. As a result, these teens may also feel anxious about socializing in new settings.

Problems with socializing may affect more extroverted, hyperactive, or impulsive teens as well. They may burst into a room and overwhelm strangers if they monopolize conversations and engage in monologues sharing more than the listener can handle. This inability to successfully socialize can significantly hamper a transitioning teen's adjustment to the new world of college.

**Make a list.** List the groups and situations that exist in your teen's everyday life in which these skills can be practiced.

**Identify unfamiliar environments.** Identify even more unfamiliar environments where you teen would need to stretch and grow, for example, weekend overnight activities sponsored by the school or a local church youth group, or summer bridge or summer school experiences that will force meeting and talking with new people.

## Explaining Strengths, Weaknesses, and Disability

It will be critical for your teen to be able to explain her strengths and weaknesses and how her disability affects learning. Being able to list and request accommodations that help her compensate is also crucial so your teen gets what she needs to have equal access to her classes. Far too many teens are unable to do these tasks when they arrive at college and meet with disability service providers or talk with teachers.

**Make a folder.** Have your teen make a folder that will accompany him to college and be a tool for self-advocacy. The

➡ **Coaching Reminder!** Before your teen attends a social function, talk with him about how to introduce himself to strangers and about the opportunities he will have to practice talking and listening and keeping the conversation going. It is also important to encourage your teen to set a very specific goal at these functions, for example: "I will introduce myself to three new people and hold several minutes of conversation with each." Depending on your teen's needs, he may want to practice these skills with you or go over a list of conversation starters (e.g., talking about sports, television shows, school, vacations, etc.) and ways to keep conversations going (e.g., asking more questions, sharing a comment or nonverbals that show interest).

folder should include a copy of the most recent report, other school records (Individualized Education Plans [IEPs], 504 plans), and some essays that he has written that answer the following questions (also have your teen practice verbally responding to the questions, too):

- What are my strengths and my weaknesses?

- What is my disability? When was it diagnosed? How does it impact my learning? How does it impact me in other areas of my life?

- What accommodations or modifications do I need to help me compensate for my disability?

- What is my learning style and what are some strategies that I know to help me learn? (These are the answers to the questions asked in the self-knowledge part of the College Readiness Survey.)

## Talking to Teachers

Now is the time to become aware of how this process will differ in college when students no longer receive services under an IEP and also to learn to advocate with professors and other faculty.

**Participate in IEP or 504 plan meetings.** If your teen is receiving special education services or accommodations, use the IEP process or 504 plan meetings to teach her about her rights and how to participate effectively in these meetings and ask for what she needs.

**Practice explaining needs.** If your teen has a regular education class teacher who doesn't understand his needs, have him practice having a conversation with this teacher, or if writing works better, help your teen write an e-mail requesting a meeting.

**⇨ Coaching Reminder!** Fight the temptation to go talk to the teacher alone or to call the school. Instead, try role playing this conversation with your teen. Let your teen use notes to guide the conversation. However, if your teen would like you to be present at the meeting, have her inform the teacher that you will coming along for support. Before the meeting, have a discussion on what role your teen wants you to play during the meeting. Sometimes, parents need to be firm that they won't be speaking and that the teen needs to speak up for herself.

## Asking for Help

At college, your teen will need to be able to recognize not only when to seek help but also how to find appropriate resources. Here are some tips to help your teen get ready now.

**Dealing with medical issues on his own.** If your teen complains of medical problems (sore throats, allergies, colds, etc.) or side effects to any medications, encourage him to take these concerns to his physician. Help your teen to make a list of his concerns and to practice what to say during the phone call or office appointment.

**Notice when your teen is trying to solve an issue on her own and meeting with limited success.** Ask your teen who in the school might be the appropriate person to talk with about this challenge. Search the high school website to learn about all the available resources. Once the resource person is identified, ask your teen if she would like to practice how to talk with this person and explain the situation.

**Make a list of resources at college.** As it gets closer to when your teen will be attending college, have him search the college's web site to find resources to address various issues, including living arrangements, health-related or emotional issues, academic supports, and disability services. Encourage your teen to bookmark these web pages and talk about when and how to use these resources.

## Learning to Disagree

Being able to disagree, voice a different opinion, or stand up for what one believes in are important skills that will be needed throughout adult life. While most teens have experienced

**Coaching Reminder!** Be on guard against the temptation to jump in and help out. This pattern can commonly develop in many families where a teen's inability to be assertive leads him to ask a parents or a sibling to act as a tutor or troubleshoot an academic problem.

conflict at home and at school prior to college, they may not have learned how to effectively disagree and present their convictions. To develop this skill, try one or all of the following:

**Talk about it instead of complaining.** Notice when your teen is complaining about someone or something, and encourage her to voice these feelings to the appropriate person. Depending on your teen's temperament, she may find this to be an overwhelming task or might relish the opportunity to face a conflict.

**Role play.** Offer the opportunity to role play various conversations in which your teen has the opportunity to disagree with your opinion. Suggest that your teen write out how he wants to express his thoughts before holding these conversations. Encourage him to express these thoughts using "I messages" that clearly express his feelings.

**Encourage disagreements within your family.** Many of us came from families that didn't model how to disagree. Be on the lookout for real opportunities when disagreements of opinions or what to do surface and try your best to model how to disagree and encourage your teen to state his opinion rather than shut down or get frustrated.

# Skill: Self-Management

Self-determined individuals not only know who they are and how to speak up for themselves but also can manage their lives independently. Individuals who have strong self-management or self-regulation skills can effectively manage any challenging situation they experience. Like the self-determined pilot who has taken off on her first solo flight, a teen with strong self-management skills can set a goal for a specific destination, draw up a well-developed flight plan, notice signs of problems and difficulties early on, and redirect herself to deal with these unexpected changes, while still reaching her goal. If emotions or other circumstances interfere with the original plan, a self-determined teen can deal with these and be persistent.

## Dealing With Emotions

Managing one's self requires that a teen manage the full range of emotions and frustrations that are a regular part of life. Many teens with ADHD or LD, however, have very low frustration tolerance and may abandon plans at the first sign of trouble or get totally derailed by their feelings. Successfully managing strong emotions requires that a teen have the ability to observe when an emotion is blocking progress. Next, he needs to handle the situation more productively. Finally, he must determine what to do to solve the problem. Try the following coaching skills to help your teen develop self-management skills.

**Seek help now if your teen has difficulties managing emotions.** Because self-management of emotions and frustrations is such

**➡ Coaching Reminder!** You may be more able to notice when your teen is dealing with a strong emotion. When the time is right, promote discussion of what is going on: "I noticed you seemed upset. What are you feeling?" Just listen and don't minimize her feelings.

Once your teen has expressed what she is feeling or what she felt, ask open-ended, curious, coaching questions to encourage problem solving: "What do you think might help you deal with this feeling?" or "How can I be of support to you right now?" Communicate in ways that validate what your teen is feeling and give a sense that you understand: "I can see that this is really frustrating to you."

Then encourage your teen to persist even though things are rough: "Can I make a suggestion? Maybe taking a break right now might help. Do you think that it might help if you go for a walk or listen to music? Then you can come back with a fresh attitude and see how things go."

an important skill for success in college and in life, be willing to admit if your teen needs more help with this now. Talk with your teen about how the challenges at college are likely to increase and learning how to cope more effectively now will make the transition better. Search together for the resources available at school and in the community that could help your teen develop better skills to become more aware of his emotions and how to manage them more effectively.

In conclusion, keep in mind that your teen's future success

may be riding on the development of these self-determination skills, so don't give up or short change him by focusing too heavily on purely academic skills. Ten years from now, it won't matter what grade he received on his World History test, but the world will notice if he can make his opinions known, handle frustrations, or if he is passionate about his career. So spend as much time as you need on these skills and when he is ready move on to the more mundane, but necessary, areas like doing laundry or scheduling doctor's appointments covered in the next chapter.

# Chapter 7
## Developing Daily Living Skills

While some problems in daily living skills may result in only minor glitches, other deficits in key skills may have dire consequences. For example, teens who have not learned how to balance life and stress may end up "burning the candle at both ends" and suffer serious physical or emotional consequences. The amount of time your teen has left in high school before taking off to college will determine whether you can work with your teen to develop these skills slowly over time or whether you are going to need to go cold turkey. When using either approach, keep in mind that it is likely that your teen will need to endure natural or parent-provided consequences in order to grow and develop new daily living skills. As you pull out the props, know that it's better to have your teen fall when there is a "parachute" attached because she is living at home rather than when she is on her own at college. So, roll up your sleeves, and let's get started!

### Skill: Self-Care

Okay, who reading this book has never had to deal with the consequences of using hot water with the wrong fabric or color or forgetting to empty tissues out of pockets when doing laundry? Raise your hand. What about being late? Oversleeping? Forgetting to exercise? The tips and ideas listed below have come directly from our work with families of college-bound teens and advice from teens who have had to do a crash course in developing these life skills.

## Doing the Laundry

Turning your white clothes pink or pulling a wool sweater out of the dryer only to find that it has shrunk to the size of a hand puppet are such common experiences, they have almost become rites of passage. It happens to the best of us when we are in a hurry, but for teens with attention-deficit/hyeractivity disorder (ADHD) or learning disability (LD), these situations can happen over and over, particularly if they don't get a complete orientation on how to do laundry. So, unless you have the resources to pay for the laundry service on campus, don't mind if your teen buys new clothes when his are dirty (yes, we hear about this approach all the time), or are prepared to do tons of dirty laundry when your teen comes home to visit, your son or daughter will need to learn how to keep up with dirty laundry.

The organizational difficulties of teens diagnosed with ADHD or LD can make problems with doing the laundry even more exaggerated. We have met teens whose roommates asked them to move out because their dirty laundry was piled all over the dorm room or suite. Or teens whose already questionable social skills were made worse when they wore terribly wrinkled, dirty, smelly clothes during midterms or finals because their stress levels kept them from doing the laundry. Don't minimize how important it can be for your teen to have lots of practice doing laundry before leaving home for college. While learning how to fit this new life task into their schedule can be tough for all college students, this new skill can be very challenging for teens diagnosed with ADHD or

LD who are also adjusting to many other new tasks. Assuming that your teen has selected this skill as one that needs to be developed before college, map out how much time your teen will have for learning this skill and then move through the following step-by-step sequence.

**Give your teen some basic instruction on doing the laundry.** Be sure to choose an approach that matches her learning style. Would it be best to have her do an Internet search and read about it? Watch a video? There are tons of videos on YouTube geared specifically to college students. Or would a demonstration work best? If so, by whom? You? An older sibling? Cousin? Relative?

**➪ Coaching Reminder!** Decide together on the actual date when you will stop being involved in teaching and your teen will be ready with the laundry. You should also ask in advance what role, if any, your teen wants you to play if you notice that laundry is piling up. Once this is determined, set your limits clearly, for example: "As of next Monday, I will no longer be including your dirty clothes in the laundry." Then be ready to shut your teen's bedroom door and fight the urge to go in and check. Remember, in a few short weeks or months, you won't have any idea if his hamper is overflowing or if he is wearing dirty, wrinkled clothes.

**Break the task up into parts.** This includes how and why you sort clothes, emptying pockets, selecting different water temperatures, selecting load sizes, cycles, and detergent options.

**Using the dryer.** Provide information about use of the dryer, including the importance of different settings, cleaning the filter, and so on.

**Create a schedule.** Design your own individualized laundry training program and lay it out on a calendar. Who will do what, when?

## Taking Medications Without Reminders

Once at college, teens with unique health issues soon discover the importance of having the skills to manage themselves with no adult around to provide support and reminders. Whether they take medication for acne, allergies, asthma, diabetes, ADHD, or other emotional issues like depression or anxiety, teens need to learn how to stay on top of their medical issues. Teens who have not fully accepted their need for medications or special medical treatments often refuse to take medications or follow treatments as prescribed when their parents aren't around. The earlier parents begin partnering with their teens to deal with these medical issues the better. Below are some tips that parents can use while teens are living at home to increase the possibility that they will understand and accept their medical needs and develop skills in taking care of any health issues.

**Let your teen take the lead.** Begin by allowing your teen to take the lead at doctor's appointments related to her health issues. The goal is to make sure your teen understands her health issues and is informed about the necessary medical treatments. Prior to appointments, have your teen think about these issues and make a list of any questions to ask.

**Address any resistance.** If your teen is resisting medical treatment, schedule a meeting with your health care professional for help in dealing with your teen's reactions. While it can be scary for a teen to refuse to take medications or follow a special diet, involving your doctor can provide you with guidance on how to handle this rebellion. Letting your teen face the consequences of his choices while still living at home may prove to be much safer than postponing this until college. Of course, if your teen has a more serious health issue, then you may not be able to totally let go. Here again, it's critical to follow your doctor's advice.

**Set up a system.** Be sure to point out any systems that you may have used to ensure that medication was taken on time or any special dietary conditions you put into place. But, remember, these may not be the one that your teen selects.

**➡ Coaching Reminder!** The first thing you will need to do to facilitate your teen's independence in taking care of his health issues is to become more aware of how you might be taking over in this area of his life. Take this time as an opportunity to change and begin to coach your teen to think of ways that she can remember to take medications or keep track of any special medical conditions. Talk about all of the tools that are available to help. These include external alarms on a cell phone or watch. Also, it's important to collaboratively create an action plan to move you out of the picture. Talk about the roles you can play as you slowly hand over the responsibility for managing medication and other treatments to your teen.

## Making Doctor Appointments and Refilling Prescriptions

Part of being responsible for managing one's health is the ability to schedule doctor's appointments and to order prescription refills. These skills are challenging for many first-year college students who routinely call their parents, who may be hundreds of miles away, when they are sick at college. Having to call the campus health center for the first time to schedule an appointment can be a quick wake-up call to adulthood for these teens. One teen we know was totally overwhelmed at the thought of doing these activities on her own at college. Soon after she started college, her parents mandated that they would no longer make calls for her prescriptions or make doctor's appointments for her. She actually broke into tears at having to take over these new responsibilities at the same time that she was learning how to be responsible for requesting her accommodations and dealing with all the other adjustments to college. She expressed quite clearly that she wished her parents would have had her practice these skills while she was in high school. She added that she "hated growing up!"

Here are some tips to help your teen get started learning how to assume these responsibilities before taking off to college.

**Create a list of doctors and medications.** Have your teen make a list of the doctors he sees and their phone numbers, as well as the names and dosages of any medication he takes. Encourage him to record this information in several places. Encourage listing what he knows about the use of each medication and any questions he may have as well.

**Learn about medical insurance.** Discuss how your medical insurance works for appointments and prescriptions and make sure that your teen has the necessary insurance information (insurer's name, policy numbers, forms for medication, etc.).

**Set up reminder systems.** Ask your teen to think about what tools she wants to use to provide reminders about ordering medications or calling for appointments. Some teens count out their pills when new prescriptions are filled and program their cell phone to provide a reminder about a week to 10 days before they will run out of their medications. Using online calendars can be a helpful reminder as well.

➥ **Coaching Reminder!** Come to an agreement as to when you will no longer be involved in helping your teen order medications or call doctors. Ask your teen what supportive role he wants you to play as you hand over the responsibility. Does he want you to model how you make calls? Provide spoken or written reminders? Meet regularly to look over the supply of medication and help him keep a calendar to remember when it is time to re-order a prescription.

## Cooking Meals and Grocery Shopping

At college, teens will have total independence over what selections they make for all of their meals and snacks or whether they eat at all. From our work with teens with ADHD or LD, we have observed issues with eating as a result of stress as well as their overall difficulties with organization and time management. We have met many teens who do not make time for meals as their lives become more stressful and other teens whose medications may cause them to skip meals and they end up binging later at night on pizza and junk food. So, it is great that your teen has identified this is one skill that needs to be a part of her personalized training program. You and your teen will be able to find a great deal of helpful information as you begin to build this new skill. The following tips may help you when developing your action plan.

**Conduct an Internet search on healthy eating for teens or on how to avoid weight gain in college.** Before teens can eat or prepare healthy meals, they need to be sure they know what types and amounts of food are suggested for teens to eat in a day.

**Seek out resources.** Look for resources at high school, online, and in your community to help your teen achieve his goals. Does the school health class have sessions on healthy eating and meal preparation? Can the school nurse offer any additional information on these topics? What about your teen's medical doctor, or are there courses at local hospitals? Are there any cooking classes geared to teens in your community?

**Create a menu.** Plan a menu for a week and practice shopping and preparing meals together.

**Look for a mentor.** This might be an older sibling or cousin who has already been to college and knows what can happen to meals and eating habits.

## Setting Up a Regular Exercise Program

Getting adequate exercise is another important skill in the area of self-care for all teens and young adults. Not only can exercise help transitioning teens avoid gaining weight, but it can

➡️ **Coaching Reminder!** If your teen's eating issues are more significant, now is the time to get more help. Have your teen do some research at school or online to learn about the various supports like Overeaters Anonymous (http://www.oa.org) or Weight Watchers (http://www. weightwatchers.com). Is the help of a therapist needed? Facing more significant eating issues now will hopefully avoid greater problems later.

also help them balance the stress they experience at college. Exercise is even more critical for teens diagnosed with learning, attention, and emotional challenges. There is ample evidence that daily aerobic activity can have significant impact on the brains of individuals in general, as well as those with specific difficulties. Exercise can improve overall attention, mood, and sleep and can lower stress level. The following are some ways you can help your teen learn to value exercise.

**Make a commitment to exercising.** Exercise yourself so that you can set an example.

**Make it enjoyable.** Ask your teen to think of ways that would make exercise more enjoyable and more likely to happen. When would it fit in the schedule? Would joining a team or a gym help? Would it help to have an exercise buddy?

**Collaboratively design a plan.** Work with your teen to form this new habit and build in regular check-ins to evaluate how things are going and what your teen is noticing on the days when he exercises and the days exercise is missed. Hopefully, by seeing the benefits on regular exercise, your teen will be more motivated and committed to keeping to the plan.

> **Coaching Reminder!** Ask your teen what role, if any, she wants you to play to support reaching exercise goals. One teen gave her mom permission to ask the following question if exercise time went by the wayside: "I noticed that you skipped exercise today, is that really what you want to do?" Because this teen gave her mom the precise words to say, she responded well to this question and didn't perceive it as nagging.

## Managing Money

Problems in money management can be commonplace for college students. Let's face it: Given the financial times we are in, families who may have had excess money for their teen to squander are a thing of the past. Unfortunately, many teens lack financial literacy skills and are, once again, placed in the position to have many temptations for spending money with no adult supervision at college. Add to this mix the reality that the cost of college has risen steadily over the last decade, and you will find that more and more teens can only go to college if they take out student loans and use credit cards. As a result, if teens aren't good at money management, when they leave college—with or without a degree—they or their parents may have accrued a great deal of debt. Despite getting a good paying job, the need to pay back large debts can prevent many young adults from breaking the cycle of overusing credit cards and living beyond their means.

Now, consider how this situation becomes even more complicated when teens are diagnosed with ADHD or LD and have trouble planning, prioritizing, keeping track of things, controlling impulses, or delaying gratification. These deficits can wreck havoc with money management when a teen is on his own in college or later in life. There is much that can be done before sending your teen to college to practice the skills needed so that he will be able to manage money well and be trusted with credit cards!

Before you begin to work with your teen on this issue, take an honest look at your money-management skills and credit card usage. We know that children learn from the models around them. This is true in all things, especially habits and attitudes toward money and debt. If you also have money-management issues, use your teen's decision to work on this goal as an opportunity to learn and change together. Use the tips below as you and your teen make a personalized plan for improving in this important skill.

**Collaboratively check out resources.** With your teen, find out what resources are available online and in your community. Most banks have staff who will meet with customers to help with money management. Nonprofit agencies in the community may have workshops and courses. Check at your church, your local YMCA, or the local community colleges.

**Build awareness.** Ask your teen to think about what her unique problems are in the area of money management or credit card usage. Greater awareness can help your teen make more specific SMART goals (see Chapter 5) to improve in money-management skills.

## Ready for Take-Off

**Look at your role.** Identify how you might be contributing to your teen's money problems. You can stop enabling your teen. Be very clear about the consequences that you will be introducing for mismanagement of money, such as large telephone bills or reckless shopping.

**Discover the power of earning.** Talk with your teen about the need to do chores or get some part-time work to earn spending money. Many teens raised in today's world have not experienced any connection between what they do and the money they have. Their parents' money may seem endless or they may not value it. If your teen needs more respect for money, now is the time to set some expectations for earning an allowance or for a part-time job.

**Create a budget.** Sound money management encourages having a budget and learning to live within this budget. What is a reasonable budget for your teen?

**Keep a log of expenses.** Once expenses are recorded, it becomes easier to see one's habits and what needs to change.

**Determine the best form for payments, purchases, and spending money.** Discuss what would work best for your teen using actual money, having a checkbook, or using an ATM card. Many of the students we worked with learned that it was better to actually work with cash and not use ATM withdrawals as a way of life. Given their disorganization and tendency not to think through what they were doing, they found that they overspent when using plastic. Money is concrete, and as it decreases in quantity and denomination, teens could see the consequences of their decisions.

**Learn about credit cards.** The new credit card laws will do much to prevent the past epidemic of college students being lured into signing up for credit cards for free T-shirts or MP3 players. If they are under 21, they will have to have an adult cosign or have evidence that they can pay their own bills. Of course, some teens will get older friends to cosign, so they may still get cards without their parents' knowledge. If you both decide that your teen can be trusted with a credit card, it may make sense to try this skill with him during high school when you can oversee what happens.

**↪ Coaching Reminder!** Work with your teen to develop a timeline for how she will become more independent in money management. If you are slowly fading your involvement, perhaps you can meet weekly to look at how budgeting is going and brainstorm solutions for better money management. If you are going cold turkey because your teen is taking off to college soon, be clear about your limits for her budget and the consequences. Also, consider whether your teen has shown you good financial responsibility as you decide on what the next step will be after high school. Many parents of teens send students off knowing that they aren't yet good at managing money, and chaos often ensues.

## Managing Stress

The right amount of stress can enhance our lives, helping us perform better and take action when needed. There are many predictable times in life when stress is heightened and can't be avoided. For example, whenever we are forced to deal with changes such as moving from the familiar to the unfamiliar (like transitioning to college or having a teen leave home) and are thrown out of our comfort zone, stress follows.

As we discussed previously, some individuals have inborn temperaments that allow them to welcome and even seek out new and novel experiences, whereas others dig in their heels and resist the inevitable changes that are part of life. In addition, some personalities seem to create their own stress, whereas others are so laid back that they don't seem to get ruffled easily. Although stress in life is unavoidable, the real problems occur when we experience chronic stress or too much stress at one time. When this happens, if we don't have the right tools, things can get out of control, our learning and behavior can be hampered, and our bodies can't cope. However, there is much that we can do to be able to manage our stress and make good decisions when things in life get stressful.

High school can be an especially stressful time for teens because of their age, the normal adolescent issues they are facing, and the pressures to fit in, look good, and do well in school. It also stands to reason that all college-bound teens, even those without any learning, attention, or emotional disabilities, will encounter additional stress as they adapt to this new world with its greater responsibilities. Many teens we meet tell us that they wished their parents hadn't shielded them from stress during high school and had helped them know more about how to prevent stress when possible and how to manage stress more effectively.

Here are some ideas to use as you and your teen develop

an action plan for this college readiness skill.

**Conduct an Internet search.** Search the Internet together on the topic of teens and stress or handling the stress of college. There are literally thousands of great websites targeted to helping young people handle stress. After checking out these sites, have your teen select some ideas that he thinks are particularly relevant for him and that he would like to learn how to implement now.

**Plan ahead to prevent stress.** Encourage your teen to engage in regular, "big-picture" planning (weekly, monthly, semester) and mark a monthly calendar to spot the really crazy times ahead. Planners that only show a day at a time or a week spread out over several pages or even those in cell phones may not give the same visual wake-up call. Schedule big school assignments and big social or sporting events on this big-picture calendar to clearly see the weeks that will be really stressful. By seeing these "crazy" times in advance, it is possible to be proactive and avoid being overwhelmed.

**Pay attention to the warning signs of stress.** When your teen begins to feel stress, encourage her to notice the feelings she is having and to ask herself why she is having them. Then set about problem-solving to decrease the stress. She needs to believe that there is a solution to the problem; be able to identify the problem; brainstorm options; pick the one that she thinks is best; and then take action.

**Keep up daily activities that help her stay well when stress hits.** Encourage your teen to practice doing the things that she knows will calm her: breathe, listen to music, exercise meditate, pray.

**Reach out to others for support.** During stress filled times it is even more important to talk to friends and family and to ask yourself, "Who are the resource people that I can go to for help?" Too many teens stay stressed because they keep their problems a secret due to pride, embarrassment, fear of judgment, and the belief that they are supposed to figure things out themselves.

➡ **Coaching Reminder!** Ask your teen to think about his usual pattern for handling stress. Think about times when your teen handled things quite well and when things didn't go so well. Ask about how not managing stress well has affected his decisions, learning, behavior, and life in general. Share your feedback in a nonjudgmental way by just describing what you have noticed. Observe if your teen has extreme difficulties coping with stress or is using nonproductive coping mechanisms, such as food, drugs, alcohol, and so on. Look for help in your community. Know that when you aren't around at college, your teen won't magically learn better stress management strategies. Now is the time to get help!

## Skill: Organization

Deficits in executive functioning skills—those higher level thinking skills that are at the heart of good organizational and time management skills—are at the root of most of the learning, attention, and self-control problems of teens with ADHD and LD. Many experts agree that underdeveloped executive functioning skills underlie the chronic difficulties these individual have keeping order in their lives. In addition to the normal activities of teenage life, teens with ADHD and LD often become so involved in outside activities to fix their academic problems that they don't have time to focus on daily life priorities, such as developing routines for the many chores they will face in college (e.g., cleaning their rooms or organizing their daily schedules).

## Keeping a Clean Room

Many teens have rooms that look chaotic at times, but having a room that is totally out of control or totally disorganized may be all too common for teens diagnosed with ADHD or LD. This pattern may have developed in your household for a number of reasons. First, you may have decided that with all of the problems you have to take on, a clean room may be low on your list of priorities. Keep in mind, however, that college roommates won't love your son or daughter like you do and won't be able or willing to ignore the devastation on the other side of the room, suite, or apartment. At some point, dealing with this issue will become important if your teen is to hold on to and find what she needs when it is needed to have life run more smoothly in college.

If you are lucky enough to have your teen admit that this is a skill that needs attention before going off to college, the following are some tips on how to coach your teen to create an action plan to work on this skill.

**Look for a reason why.** Ask your teen what he thinks causes the disorganization in his room and with his possessions. By coaching your teen to think more about what causes the problems, he will be more able to find an effective solution.

**Agree on a definition.** What does a "clean" room looks like? Since your teen is still living in your house, you should have some say in this definition, but you have to also realize that she may have a very different definition and tolerance for mess than you do.

**Create an action plan.** Frequently, this is where teens with ADHD or LD get frustrated. Instead of being able to come up with a plan, their emotional reactions to how huge the mess is and not knowing where to start block their problem-solving skills. Or they get lost trying to think of the perfect plan and perfect way to clean a room, rather than taking the first step. Just asking about the small steps involved in cleaning a room may allow your teen to create a plan. Remember, how you would clean the room is not important. You are coaching, not teaching. There is no right way to get started. If your teen gets stuck, suggest getting some additional ideas by asking his friends how they go about cleaning their rooms or asking an older sibling or cousin for help.

**Make a list of supplies.** This may include garbage bags for trash or old clothes; boxes, plastic tubs, or containers to keep things in; and other cleaning supplies. Encourage your teen to store this list on his computer so that he will have a copy handy at college when he goes to buy supplies when he gets there.

**Schedule a time for each step.** Grounding the plan in time is the key to making it happen. What time is really available during the week, even if there might only be 10 to 15 minutes? What time is available during the weekend?

**Decide on a strategy.** For example, does your teen want to start by category or by location? (Category: find all the clean clothes and put those away, then all the dirty clothes, then the school stuff, CDs, and video games. Location: clear off the bed, the desk, the floor.)

**⮑ Coaching Reminder!** Ask your teen what role you can play in helping her follow through on the plan? Does your teen want you to be present to be of support, to remind her, or to check when the job is done? To be sure you are part of the solution, tell your teen what your bottom line is regarding the state of her room and what you are no longer willing to tolerate and to do. Your bottom line will depend on how much time before your teen takes off for college. If you have more time, you might choose to set a firm rule and provide a consequence that will help your teen form this new habit, like "If you don't keep your room clean (according to the agreed-upon definition), you will not be able to go out for the weekend until it is picked up." Or you might say, "From now on my willingness to give you money to buy new things like clothes, video games, CDs, etc., will be dependent on whether you demonstrate that you can keep your room clean." Finally, ask your teen to think about how she will keep order in the room once it is clean. Once again, encourage a daily time to straighten things rather than a weekly or monthly big clean-up. The goal is for your teen to learn to slow down and prevent a mess rather than live in the all-or-nothing pattern that led to the chaos in the room in the first place.

## Keeping Track of Possessions

Problems with keeping track of possessions often tend to go hand-in-hand with problems keeping one's room in order. If things like keys, wallets, cell phones, CDs, homework assignments, school books, sports equipment (the list goes on and on) don't have a predictable home, they can get lost temporarily or forever. Many families and teens we know have spent a great deal of money and time and experienced much suffering because of the teens' constant habits of losing things, not being able to find them, and having to habitually replace them. This common problem causes many parents to become chronic enablers as they take over reminding, nagging, and picking things up, all in an attempt to prevent the recurring nightmares. The following tips are provided for how to coach your teen to develop an action plan for this skill.

**Determine the why.** Encourage your teen to be curious about this pattern, and remember, do not be judgmental. Say, "Truly (your teen's name), I know this pattern frustrates and embarrasses you, but when you really think about it, I am curious, how do you think you keep losing your _____ (fill in the blank)?" Share your observations and theories that you think contributes to this pattern. Make a list.

**Look at what works.** Now, ask your teen to think of some possession that he has been able to keep track of or a time when he seemed better able to keep track of things. Ask, "I am curious, what do you think helps you know where your (fill in the blank) is? You have done a great job keeping track of it." Or "Remember that time (specific example) when you had a whole week when you didn't lose anything, what do you think helped you do that?" The possible strategies for improving this skill are tucked away in the examples of success that you and your teen can recall. Share what you think may have helped. Make a list.

**Brainstorm ideas.** These might include setting up a home for the possessions that keep getting lost. Select a specific location in a space that makes sense to your teen. Would a basket by the door work? Or a shelf in his room? Be creative. Some teens have created a home or parking lot for their keys, phone, and wallet in the bathroom!

**Create a reminder system.** Does your teen need reminders to remember to use the new home or parking lot? What about having a reminder programmed into the cell phone that goes off at a logical time and asks, "Where is your stuff?" What about using a Google calendar (http://www.google.com/googlecalendar/about.html) to send multiple reminders during the day asking, "Do you know where your _____ is?"

**⤷ Coaching Reminder!** Ask your teen for advice on what role she wants you to play as the plan is implemented. As always, in a more gradual approach, you can slowly fade your role. But be clear about your bottom line. Are you still going to buy another iPhone if your teen loses the one he got for his birthday? No, we hope not. Or what will you do if your teen calls and says she forgot to bring money to school? Remember that soon you won't be nearby to fix the consequences of your teen forgetting or losing possessions.

## Skill: Time Management

Difficulty with time management is most often directly related to having ADHD or LD, and the fact that these disorders contribute to a teen having no concept of time, an impaired ability to judge the passing of time, or not even knowing what time it is. These teens lose all sense of time and can become lost in their own world. Distractibility also contributes to getting off task and contributes to an inability to stick to a schedule despite their best efforts. These deficits account for a student's failure to complete tasks on schedule, to get to classes and appointments on time, and to have difficulty getting to bed or waking on the morning.

### Getting More Sleep

In general, teenagers don't get enough sleep. Most experts find that the biological clock for an adolescent gets pushed back later and later. However, their bodies still require 8½ to 9½ hours of sleep. Some teens diagnosed with ADHD or LD may tend to be night owls who get more alert and attentive as the sun sets. For some, this pattern is related to their tendency to procrastinate doing homework and studying, and they begin much too late in the day and stay up late to finish work that is due the next morning. For others, this habit results from wanting to do their school work late at night when the house is quiet, causing them to not go to bed until the wee hours of the morning. Or they may have trouble quieting their thoughts or emotions and are not able to fall asleep even when their bodies are fatigued.

If your son or daughter is like Kathy, whom we met in Chapter 4 and has these challenges, you may have fallen into the pattern of acting as your teen's human alarm clock, just like Kathy's father did. Deep sleepers or teens who may have just fallen asleep a few short hours before it is time to get up may not hear even the loudest alarm. It might take a parent bellowing or pulling back the covers or, if they are courageous, shaking them awake. If teens haven't learned how to independently fall asleep and wake up before going to college, serious problems can result, including missed early morning classes. If the professor takes attendance and has strict policies, then missing morning classes can lower a student's grade, not to mention the impact it has on the student's emotions. Sometimes, college students feel so embarrassed about oversleeping that they can't face returning to classes they've missed. So they opt instead to quit going and get very a low grade, or even fail the class. We have even encountered teens who have slept through exams because, after days of going without adequate rest, their bodies just crashed.

Here are some tips to help you and your teen create an action plan to improve going to bed at a reasonable time and awakening independently.

**Check for sleep disorders.** If you and your teen have wondered about the possibility of a full-blown sleep disorder, now is the time, before college, to check this out. Encourage your teen to call her doctor and find out who the experts are in your community in the area of sleep disorders. Many local hospitals also have sleep study centers.

**Analyze the reasons.** Ask your teen to analyze what he thinks are some of the reasons that getting to sleep at a reasonable hour and waking up independently are problematic. Pinpointing his unique set of reasons is the first step in figuring out a personalized plan for improvement.

**Check out caffeine.** Ask your teen about caffeine intake and use of energy drinks. These legal substances are popular with teens and young adults and can be used in unhealthy quantities as a way to deal with busy times and often result in difficulty falling asleep at night.

**Investigate stimulant use.** If your teen is on medication for attention issues, ask her doctor if it is possible that her sleep problems are a side effect of the medication. In addition, you may need to have a heart-to-heart talk about how she is using it. Doctors frequently give specific orders not to take these medications past a certain time. We know teens who deliberately took their medication later in the evening or took more doses in the day to be able to handle busy social and academic schedules. If this is the case, have your teen meet with the prescribing doctor for an honest talk. Even if your teen is not on medication for ADHD, ask if he has ever tried using it. Unfortunately, stimulant medication is frequently bought, traded, and abused by young adults, so open the door for this honest conversation, just in case there are other reasons for your teen's sleep problems.

**Find out what works.** Ask your teen to think about times when going to sleep and getting up were easier. Maybe sleep is better when your teen exercises or when she is on top of school work and doesn't feel worried or anxious. Was it easier to wake up when there was something exciting going on at school or if a friend was driving that day? Identify what seems to help her fall asleep and get up more easily.

**Learn how to fall asleep.** Check out the websites listed in resources section or do a search with your teen to read about what experts say can help a teen fall asleep and wake up.

**Set an alarm for going to sleep.** Ask your teen to think about when "lights need to go out" for him to get much needed sleep. Would it help to set the alarm on the cell phone to go off each night an hour before the agreed-upon lights-out time?

**Create a nighttime routine.** Ask your teen to think about a nighttime routine that would help her unwind and make the morning go more smoothly. When should homework and studying be done? What about getting everything ready for the next day? Would it help to have some downtime right before it is time for lights out, like reading or listening to music? Should your teen leave his cell phone somewhere other than in the bedroom so that sleep won't be disrupted and there won't be the temptation to text or call a friend? Encourage your teen to create a nighttime checklist and post it in a prominent place to guide his use of time as he prepares for bed.

**Find the ideal alarm.** Explore ideas for alarms that will do the job at waking her up. Would a clock radio set on a loud station work better than an alarm? How about several alarms staggered at different times and in different places in the room? A number of companies make extra-loud alarms. Some college students with extreme difficulty waking up have found that vibrating alarms for individuals who are deaf or have hearing loss to be helpful.

➡ **Coaching Reminder!** Ask your teen what role you can play as this skill is worked on. Again, if you are able to do a gradual approach to skill development, you can start playing the role of reminding, checking, and then eventually letting go. If your teen is almost ready for college, you may choose to go cold turkey and let natural consequences happen right away. The bottom line is, you cannot be your teen's alarm clock, unless of course you plan to continue doing this when he is in college. Don't laugh. We actually have met college students who admitted that their mother or father still called them to wake them up because this problem was such a big deal. So, chances are that you may need support to let go and allow your teen to miss the bus or even to miss school on important days and learn to face the consequences of the choices she made the night before. As hard as this may be, just remember that in a few short, years, months, weeks, and maybe for some of you, days, you won't be around to bail your teen out. Making mistakes while still at home where you are there to help process the reasons for what happened and make a new plan of action is surely a safer way for your teen to learn than when you are miles away.

## Keeping a Balanced Schedule

The schedule of daily life for high school students has a lot of built-in structure owing to the predictability that exists. During the week there is little unstructured time for teens to make decisions; the only unstructured time that typically exists is on the weekends. But then again, depending on the teen's life, sports, volunteer activities, jobs, chores (if any), homework, and social time fill up the 48 hours before the tightly structured weekday starts all over again.

As you are well aware, the daily life of the college student is totally different, with much more unstructured time and opportunity for choice. College students spend fewer hours in class, and there are different schedules for different days with larger chunks of open blocks of time during the week and evenings as well as weekends. Most teens come to college with little or no practice in creating their own structure and learning how to find the delicate balance between play, school work, classes, life chores, down time, time for eating, time for sleeping, and so on. If college students don't design a balanced weekly schedule throughout the semester, they can fall into patterns of all-or-nothing living. During the weeks when nothing is due, teens in college often fill their time with play, downtime, or social activities. Then when midterms and final exams hit, they get totally focused on school, catching up on readings and work that had been assigned for months and pulling all-nighters to cram for test or rush to finish papers and projects. Teens with ADHD or LD can fall into these same patterns without realizing that, because of their difficulties learning, they might not be as successful at completing all the readings or functioning without sleep when it is time to get in gear with academics.

To prepare to handle stress in college, it would be helpful if all teens, but especially those diagnosed with ADHD or LD, could practice how to create a balanced daily and weekly schedule. Your son or daughter has realized this is a skill to work on, so use the ideas below to coach your teen to develop an action plan to follow during the remaining time in high school.

**Describe what a balanced life would look like.** Ask your teen, "If you had a magic wand and you could have the perfectly balanced day or week, what would the schedule look like?" What activities are excluded or included in this dream? Does the dream of a balanced life have more time to chill and do nothing? Does it have her getting work done earlier in the day or the week?

**Make a list.** What would it take to make this dream a reality? Do some of the activities that your teen is involved in have to go to make more room for down time, sleep, exercise, and social time? Or do some of the distracting time-filler activities have to go or be limited, like TV, surfing the web, visiting social networking sites, playing video game?

**Get help.** Does your teen need help limiting computer time or time on social networking sites, gaming sites, or chat rooms? We did an Internet search and found nearly 30,000 sites specializing in software that can block access to specific Internet sites. In our experience, more and more students tell us they totally get sidetracked by Internet sites that are more fun to visit than the work or chores they have to do. Some have acknowledged that they have full-blown addictions!

**Review the school schedule.** Does your teen need to consider using time during the day in study hall at school or special resource support differently so that her dream life can come true?

**Create a master schedule.** Many experts on time management start with the same suggestion: Create a master schedule to look at the time that is already committed each day and week and what occupies the remaining time. Sometimes this visual depiction of life speaks more clearly to your teen about what needs to change and how much time is being wasted or spent on activities that aren't really of value. Suggest that your teen make an hourly schedule that represents his life right now. Mark out classes, travel time to and from school, meals, sleep, sports, recurring meetings, appointments, and so on. Find where the unstructured or open blocks of time really are and count up how much open time there really is. What could be added to the day or the week, and what does he feels needs to be taken away?

⬆ **Coaching Reminder!** After he designs an action plan for a more balanced life, ask your teen what role he wants you to play. What should you do if you see him choosing a path that will not bring about the dream of a balanced life? Also, don't forget to determine when you will meet to evaluate how the new master plan for the day and the week is working. Remind your teen that in a few short years, months, or weeks, he will have to the responsibility for designing how to use all the open time periods in the day at college. Practice now will make him much more ready. Be clear to your teen about your limits and what old patterns you refuse to keep doing when he chooses not to balance life.

**Create a more balanced schedule.** Now the real work begins. Encourage your teen to decide what small steps she can take each day to make her life more balanced. Does your teen need some downtime each day to do something that she loves, like drawing, painting, playing an instrument, exercising? Or is your teen good at doing what she loves but avoiding responsibilities? Maybe your teen needs to come right home after school, avoid the TV or computer, and get right to doing school work on daily assignments and long-term assignments. Have your teen design a plan for how she might live in a more balanced way on the weekends starting with the after-school period on Fridays to Sunday night

## Being On Time

For many teens (and adults) with ADHD and LD, being on time to events and appointments is challenging. Many times chronic lateness is directly related to having no concept of time or the ability to judge time. Teens with ADHD are often unable to keep track of what time it is and to stop what they are doing to get to the destination without being distracted. Some individuals who are chronically late are so charming that their friends and family just laugh it off and accept their loved one's pattern of lateness. For many individuals, this perpetual pattern of not being on time causes shame, leads others to judge them harshly, and creates missed opportunities only adding to their stress. Of course, parents, relatives, and friends of chronically late individuals can frequently "pick up the slack" and just fall into the role of reminding, nagging, or even lying about the time.

In high school, the tight schedule with 2 to 3 minutes between classes can prevent the most social, easily distracted teen from being late, but when friends and families make appointments or gather for social activities these teens can struggle to be on time. Once in college, this tight class schedule with bells to signal how much time to get to the next class will be gone. There will be a new group of strangers who won't immediately have "the scoop" about your teen's chronic lateness problem, which can turn what was an accepted pattern at home and with friends into a larger issue that ruins friendships and causes many difficulties.

Your son or daughter has recognized that this is a skill that needs to be improved before college. The list below can help the two of you have a coaching discussion to create an action plan.

➡ **Coaching Reminder!** Discuss with your teen why she wants to be able to be on time. Maybe she values friends and feels embarrassed when everyone has to wait for her. Ask how remembering this reason can help her break the old patterns that lead to lateness. After this discussion, work with your teen to design the role you will play in supporting her efforts to learn to be on time. Get advice on what helps and what doesn't. Decide what you feel you need to stop doing because it is enabling. Be clear with your teen about what you will no longer do and why. Be ready to allow your teen to experience the natural consequences that will likely happen if she is late as you move out of the roles you may have had at reminding, explaining her behavior to others, or nagging.

**Look for patterns.** Ask your teen to think about what leads to the pattern of being late. Share what you have noticed without judging, knowing that your teen wants to change this habit. Ask your teen how she knows what time it is. Often, individuals who are chronically late don't like to wear watches and prefer letting life unfold rather than living to a strict schedule. While they may be much better at living in the moment—a skill that many wish they had—they tend not to tune into the world's clock.

**Decide on a tool.** Choose a tool that your teen would be willing to use to make himself more aware of time. Would he be willing to buy a watch that beeps or vibrates on the half hour, like the WatchMinder (http://www.watchminder.com)? Or what about using his phone to provide repeating alarms at intervals before the time of a scheduled event?

Now that you and your teen have a plan and new skills to make daily life with its numerous responsibilities more manageable, let's move on to the work of improving study skills and overall academic performance at college where the work will be much more difficult.

# Chapter 8
## Improving Academic and Study Skills

A familiar comment we hear repeatedly from many first-year college students diagnosed with attention-deficit hyperactivity disorder (ADHD) or learning disability (LD) is that they had NO CLUE how hard classes were going to be at a 4-year college. Whether the student is a new freshman coming straight out of high school or a transfer student from a community college, many first-year students who have learning and attention challenges can hit the wall academically. So, many of these students experience a rude awakening when they receive their midterm grades. It is only then that they realize that something has to change, but they are not always clear on how to make the necessary changes or where to find the resources that will help them.

Don't get us wrong. We've certainly met teens who learned early on that they had to work much harder than everyone else to get the grades they did. Frequently, these young adults diagnosed as having a learning disability at younger ages discovered that learning certain subjects didn't come easily. Their past successes were due, in large part, to their innate ability, the fact that their more obvious problems led them to receive help, and their extraordinary determination to succeed. Some teens tell us that to be successful in high school or community college, they had to read assignments three and four times to understand them. Many, like the students you met earlier in this guide, admit to sacrificing their social lives in high school or community college and did whatever it took to get good grades. Oftentimes, these teens have had formal accommodations and received formal as well as informal support in the school. They may discover that working harder isn't working anymore. Eventually, given all of the large assignments at a 4-year college, teens with this pattern learn that there aren't enough hours in a day to read and reread all of their assignments, to make flash cards for every subject, to recopy their notes, or to use any other time-consuming study strategy that brought success in the past. Some discover that even their accommodations aren't enough to allow them to deal with the new academic expectations. Some seek out more resources, whereas others, unfortunately, leave college temporarily either by their own choice or by earning poor grades that lead to probation or make them ineligible to continue. For some students, the challenges are so great that they leave college permanently.

Even though parents do not directly impact academic skill areas, we know that many of you are still overseeing your teen's school work in some fashion or other and making recommendations based on your experiences at school or in the workplace. Therefore, it is important not only that you learn about the host of new and more sophisticated study skills that college students need to be successful, but that you also understand why some of the skills your teenager is using now won't be enough for success in college. It is our hope that after reading this chapter, you will be able to influence your teen to consider some of these techniques—even if he is getting good grades in high school—to ensure that college will go more smoothly for him. Maybe you will even be able to encourage your teen's teachers to provide more direct instruction in these important skills.

# Skill: Self-Knowledge

The key to success in college for a student with special needs is often the degree of self-knowledge and perseverance that she has gained over the years in high school. If a student is already aware of her learning style and knows when and where she studies best, rather than trying to figure these things out in a new environment, she will be way ahead of the game. In addition, students need to be able to persevere at challenging assignments on their own at college when they have lots of competing activities. If your teen has decided these are areas she needs to develop before college, the following tips may help her as she develops action plans for these skills.

## Knowing Your Learning Style

Not all people learn the same way. While some experts have argued about whether learning style differences really exist, other experts suggest our styles are unique and that matching teaching and learning activities to one's style can increase learning. Many of the teens we worked with have told us that they wish they had fully understood how they learned and studied best before coming to college. Instead many said they spent their first semester using trial and error to figure their style out in preparing for their first exams. Use the tips below to help your teen become more aware of his learning style.

**Look for preferences.** Does your teen tend to learn better or prefer a more visual approach to learning and seem to remember better if there are pictures, diagrams, graphs, or charts? Does he tend to learn best if the information is spoken? Does your teen tend to like to have things explained or like to use audiobooks? Does your teen seem to like to be more active when learning new information by talking about what was learned, reteaching it, studying with others, demonstrating it, drawing, or writing information?

**Review previous evaluations.** Encourage your teen to meet with the professional who conducted her previous evaluation or with the special education teacher at her school. Ask questions about her learning style preferences.

**Observe and reflect.** While some of this "style" information might be hidden in the diagnostic report, sometimes it is best learned through observation and reflection. Ask your teen to think about the following: How did he study for a quiz or a test that went well? What preferences in learning might be hidden under this successful study method? Think of a recent time when he did poorly on a paper or a quiz. What methods of study were used and what might have worked better?

**Keep a journal.** Try various strategies and evaluate how different techniques worked. Have your teen try different methods like listening to an audiobook or watching a video to see if this helps her gain information about a topic. She also might create graphics, pie charts, or cartoon-like illustrations to accompany notes from class and record whether these enhance her ability to remember material for the test.

**Go online.** Learn more about learning styles or take a quiz online. Lots of information can be found online or in books devoted to this topic. Take the brief quiz at http://www.ldpride.net/learning-style-test-b.html or on another site to get started.

➡ **Coaching Reminder!** When the opportunity presents itself, use coaching questions targeted at helping your teen analyze her learning style. If your teen does particularly well on a test or an assignment, ask her to think about whether she studied in ways that better matched her style than when she did poorly on an exam.

## Figuring Out When and Where to Study

In addition to knowing about learning style and learning preferences, college students can benefit from knowing which study environments work best for them and when their peak times for quality attention occur. College will offer many options for studying that teens have not experienced in high school. With no adult around, they can choose to study late into the night past the time their parents would have forced them to turn the lights out. Friends will invite them to study at coffee shops, in study groups, in the lounge, in their dorms, and a host of other tempting environments. If a teen doesn't really know what time of day and what environment work best for him, much time can be wasted at college figuring this out. Once again, most college classes with only two or three exams or one large paper or project making up the grade don't have a large margin for error.

To create an action plan for this skill, your teen can try some or all of the following tips to gather information on when and where to study.

**Review past study sessions.** Review and reflect on successful and unsuccessful study sessions. This is an extremely important tool and your teen can use the information from his high school experiences rather than waiting to see what works at college.

**Create a journal.** Analyze and document whether the study environment or time of day used for studying was a key factor in whether the study session paid off or not.

**Make a list.** List all the possible study environments (tried and untried) and rate them as to whether this setting has been or might be helpful for studying.

**Create a master schedule.** Make a master schedule of her day and identify when there are open times at school or at home for studying and doing school work. Next, rate each block as to how productive this period of time has been or would be for studying and homework. Discuss together the reasons for the rating and decide what time of day is best and worst for your teen to study.

**⤷ Coaching Reminder!** Ask your teen to summarize what he learned about his favorite types of study environments and his best times for studying and doing different types of tasks. It isn't unusual for a person to have a best time for tasks that take a great deal of concentration, like early morning, late at night, or in the middle of the day. What is a reasonable amount of time for your teen to work? Can he really sit for several hours, or would shorter study periods interspersed with short breaks work better?

## Accepting Challenging Assignments

The ability to keep working even when an assignment is not very motivating is seen by researchers as an important quality found in many successful college students. This ability is probably very important for success in life as well. Right now you may be able to encourage, support, or even force your teen to keep at it when she would prefer to avoid a task altogether or just quit out of sheer frustration. However, the truth is that in a few years or maybe even months, you won't be around to supervise your teen and ensure that she can hang in there and not be lured into procrastinating by other more exciting activities. Try some of the following tips to work on this skill.

**Look for a pattern.** Identify the types of tasks that your teen finds most challenging and talk together about why this pattern might exist. Sometimes these tasks are directly rubbing up against your teen's diagnosed disability.

**Keep a journal.** Keep a journal for a week and record observations of what types of tasks were challenging and what he was thinking and feeling when trying to complete these tasks.

**Review these observations.** Go over these observations with your teen and help her create a list of challenging tasks and the reasons why they are difficult. Were the tasks all in one subject area or of the similar type? Were problems related to not understanding? Not reading directions? Not having adequate notes from class? Being too tired? Being in the wrong study environment or other reasons that you and your teen have discovered?

# Ready for Take-Off

**Generate a new plan of action.** For example, encourage your teen to do the following:

- Go to tutoring or study hall to work on homework; that way, a teacher will be nearby to help if he runs into difficulty.
- Set a time limit on how long she will try working on a problem task before taking a break or calling a friend for help.
- Find all the resources available at school or online for completing tasks that are challenging.

**Make it fun.** Help your teen think of some way to make doing the task more fun or rewarding. One student chose to do his least favorite tasks at a bookstore where he could sit in a cushy chair and sip on a flavored coffee. Another gave herself a reward of 10 minutes on Facebook for every 50 minutes she worked on a paper she found challenging.

➡ **Coaching Reminder!** Help your teen realize that some tasks are difficult and there is no simple solution for making them easier or more fun. However, facing such tasks is made more tolerable if your teen can create thoughts or incentives that are motivating. Brainstorm ways your teen can create some incentives by matching his long-term dream for the future. For example, one teen we knew had a very difficult time with foreign languages. Knowing that taking this class was necessary for a degree, she gave herself a pep talk and reminded herself of her long-term plan of being a psychologist. She simply wrote herself a note stating, "This class will help you graduate and reach your dreams." This positive thought replaced her negative thought, "I hate memorizing Spanish vocabulary words."

# Skill: Study Skills

Teens transitioning to college frequently have a long list of study skills they wish they had learned before coming to college. These include how to study, how to take notes in large lecture classes, how to handle multiple long-term assignments, and how to handle the voluminous amount of reading that is assigned in several classes. It is likely that you are reading this chapter because your teen has identified that improvement is needed in some of the skills in this section of the College Readiness Survey. At this point, your role will be to help him set SMART goals and create, and then follow, an action plan to improve in this area. In addressing each of the skills, we will share more about how the skill is used at college and provide ideas and resources that you and your teen can use to learn more about the specific skills your teen needs to work on.

## Managing Reading Assignments

Learning directly from reading is a method used in many college classes. Unlike high school, where readings are discussed in class, college classes frequently touch upon the readings in a more abstract way. Professors may synthesize multiple reading assignments on a topic in a class lecture but still ask very specific questions about each reading on the exams. While most high school classes do not have lengthy reading assignments, some subjects do require teens to read textbooks and novels. For students whose reading or attention disabilities affect their ability to read quickly and comprehend what they read, even these reading assignments are challenging to complete. Many students have told us that the only way they were able to complete assignments in high school was to stay up very late reading and, oftentimes, rereading assignments. Some students tell us that their parents actually read assignments to them because this approach allowed for better comprehension and more timely completion of work. Others admit with embarrassment that they never completed reading assignments in the past.

Managing time to stay on top of reading assignments is an important skill for your teen to develop while in high school. Try some or all of the following tips to help your teen develop this skill.

**Put it on the schedule.** As part of setting up a study schedule, encourage your teen to look at the available time she has each day and on the weekends and to decide which blocks of time would be best for completing reading assignments. When is her attention at its peak? If she is on medication to improve attention span, shouldn't reading assignments (and all homework) be done at a time when the medication is working?

**Break large reading assignments into daily goals.** For example, a 200-page novel that is due in 4 weeks could be broken into smaller more manageable daily assignments of 10 pages each for 20 days.

**Consider a study group.** Would your teen do better at staying on top of reading assignments if he could form a study group of friends who read together and discuss the readings?

**Talk with the teacher.** Suggest that your teen meet with her teacher for advice on how to approach the assigned readings more efficiently and for clarification of the key information the teacher wants students to gain from the assignment. Once again, this skill of talking directly with teachers can serve your teen well in the future at college.

## Taking Notes From Reading Assignments

Many teens tell us that they did very well in high school or community college without having to take notes from reading assignments. In fact, some teens confess that they never even completed many of their reading assignments before coming to college because the details of the assignments were discussed directly in class. These teens experience both frustration and shock when they realize that college professors typically won't review all reading assignments in depth in class yet will include questions from these assignments on their exams. As a result, many first-year college students must scramble to figure out what is important in the readings and how to keep track of important information.

It is great that your teen has rated this skill as one to work on while still in high school. Try suggesting some or all of the following tips to improve your teen's note-taking skills during reading.

**Research various note-taking techniques.** A very popular technique is the SQRW method (see http://www.education.com/reference/article/SQRW-reading-taking-notes-textbooks/). This method allows the student to use the titles, subtitles, and visual materials in the assignment to create a purpose for reading and to come up with some questions that guide reading and note-taking. Conduct a search on YouTube and check out the many videos on note-taking while reading.

**Match note-taking to learning style.** If your teen decides that he needs to write some notes as a way to recall the key information, what method will he use? Is typing or writing the best mode of taking notes? Should your teen consider making an audio file of what he has read along with some visual notes? Would it be easier to make a PowerPoint of the key information from a reading assignment?

**Use technology.** If your teen's handwriting is illegible and typing is laborious, you might consider looking into some of the scanning devices (e.g., http://www.wizcomtech.com/) that make note-taking easier or look into using dictation software such as Dragon Naturally Speaking (http://www.nuance.com/naturallyspeaking/).With this software your teen can dictate the notes from the readings, and the computer types what is said. Your teen can then format the document into nicely typed notes that are in her words.

**Make it visual.** If visual information is your teen's preferred way to organize information, then he might consider making a visual map, a table, or a graph of the important information. Again, use the Internet to search for ways to take notes visually. One such program is Inspiration (http://www.inspiration.com).

## Taking Usable Class Notes

Most first-year college students we know have limited or virtually no experience taking notes and learning in lecture classes. Given the smaller class size in high school and community colleges, many teens become comfortable with learning in a discussion-oriented setting. However, at many (although not all) colleges, classes may consist of large lectures of 50 to 100 or more students. In these lecture-based classes the professor, who is an expert in the subject area, talks during the class period with little or no time available for discussion or questions and answers. It is common for the professor to supplement the lecture by showing PowerPoint slides, which are then posted on the course website after the class (to encourage attendance). Many first-year students tell us how hard it is for them to learn and take notes in this more passive learning environment. For some the struggle is very basic. They have trouble just sitting still and remaining attentive when there is no interaction. Others find the language and vocabulary being used unfamiliar, so they struggle at grasping meaning as they try to decipher what is being said. When the students try to take notes, without the benefit of the available PowerPoint slides, many students, even those without learning and attention challenges, struggle at writing down the key points being covered. Even if the professor emphasizes the key points, students can't keep up with writing down the important details that are connected to these key points. This is one skill that many students wish they had practiced before coming to college. Since your teen has identified this skill as one to work on, it is great that she can research and experiment with various note-taking strategies while still in high school. To address this skill, encourage your teen to try the following tips.

**Look for help at school.** Identify all the resources available at school for learning more about taking complete notes in lecture classes. The guidance counselor, transition specialist, special education teacher, and librarian are good places to start.

**Conduct an Internet search.** Our search on "taking notes in a lecture" brought 7,770,000 hits. Most of these sites make the following suggestions: Taking notes begins before the student attends the class and continues after class. This includes reviewing the notes and readings from the previous class as well as checking the course syllabus to become familiar with what is going to be discussed. Going to class already aware of the vocabulary and key concepts that will be covered can make listening easier. Creating a list of questions before the class can also guide listening and improve focus.

**Decide on a format for recording notes.** Once again, the student's preference should guide him. Will a linear system of taking notes using a traditional outline really work? Or does your teen do better with bullet points and indentations to separate main ideas from details? Some note-taking systems, like the Cornell Method, suggest making two columns, the left column for the main points or key questions guiding the lecture and the right column for more details and explanations. The books listed in the resource section at the end of this guide provide more strategies for improving note-taking. Most systems encourage students to not write full sentences or every word, skipping filler words like "and" or "the" and only writing down key words and phrases.

**Talk to the teacher.** Most resources suggest that the student spend some time soon after taking notes to summarize what the key points of the lecture are and to make a list of any questions that she might have. Visiting the teacher in a one-to-one setting to review questions may be good practice for how your teen will interact with professors in college.

**Use technology.** For some students with learning and attention disabilities note-taking is nearly impossible. In such cases using available technologies and accommodations may be necessary. Find out about the latest devices by checking with your county's Vocational Rehabilitation Assistive Technology Center, the special education teacher, or your teen's school transition specialist. Would your teen benefit from asking permission to use a digital tape recorder to supplement or take the place of written notes? Or a laptop? This might be good preparation because many colleges allow or even mandate students to bring laptops to class. Your teen can also check out the latest note-taking technology, such as the Pulse Smart Pen (http://www.livescribe.com/). This relatively inexpensive pen uses special notebook paper and synchronizes what is being said to the exact letter that was written at that point in the lecture. The student doesn't have to worry about missing key details: He can go back later, tapping the pen at the point on the page when he lost the lecture, and the pen will play back the words that were spoken. With this pen and digital recorders, your teen can download the audio version of the lecture and make an audio file and listen to it over again. The pen allows the student to download the actual written notes and listen to the audio over again and modify the notes on the computer.

**Request class notes.** Would your teen benefit by having a copy of the teacher's notes or a classmate's notes as an accommodation? Some students find this accommodation critical because they cannot listen, remember, and write legibly.

## Reading Critically

Many teens may become overwhelmed when reading a textbook or even a novel that has been assigned for school. They may have no idea how to sort out what is important from what is not important. While this may not be a skill that is required very much during high school, it is critical in college, where professors can assign hundreds of pages of reading a week and require several textbooks for one class. Multiply this reality by five classes, and it is easy to understand why so many first-year college students become overwhelmed and have problems deciding what to focus on when completing reading assignments. This skill is directly related with the skill of taking notes when reading. Unless your teen has a method for sorting out the key information or the "meat" from the less important information, or the "potatoes," she will be confused at deciding what notes to write or what to remember. This skill and the previous skills are related, and your teen may choose to work on them together. The following tips will help your teen work on this important skill.

**Consider audiobooks.** Think about whether hearing the book on tape or having it read by text-reading software would allow for better comprehension of what is important. Some audiobooks can be purchased to replace books that your teen has to read. Text-reading software allows a computerized voice to read an electronic or Word document of a book or reading assignment.

**Survey other information for clues.** When reading textbooks, use the table of contents and the heading for sections to sort out the important concepts from the lesser concepts and see how the ideas fit together. Check the syllabus to see if there are any objectives written for the class or the specific lecture for which the readings are assigned. Is there a study guide? Are there questions at the end of the chapter that will provide a clue about what the key information is?

**Use the SQRW method.** Use the SQRW method for note-taking mentioned earlier (http://www.education.com/reference/article/SQRW-reading-taking-notes-textbooks). This method presents two steps to be taken before reading that help the reader determine what is important. The survey (S) step encourages the student to first do a "big picture" view of the reading assignment by looking at titles, subtitles, headings, visuals (pictures, tables, and graphs), and the chapter summary. Once the book is surveyed, the reader is encouraged to make up questions (Q) based on the information gleaned during the survey step. Be sure to check out the books listed in the resource guide at the end of this book for other strategies your teen might use to become more skilled at reading critically.

**Meet with the teacher.** If the book, the syllabus, and the class notes don't provide any clues to help determine what's important, encourage your teen to meet with the teacher and ask for advice on what her expectations should be for the reading assignments. Also, encourage your teen to meet with any resource teachers—or even the school counselor—who might be able to teach him more about strategies for critical reading. See the resource guide at the back of this book for more information on reading technology.

**Use summaries or watch a DVD.** We know that many teachers cringe at this idea, but we do think Cliff Notes, doing an Internet search on a topic of a novel, or watching a DVD can help students with reading disabilities get the big picture before they attack a novel or a lengthy assignment (not instead of reading the entire book). Encourage your teen to talk with the teacher about using these tools to supplement reading assignments.

## Learning to Write, Edit, and Rewrite Papers

Parents and teens with learning or attention challenges often develop enabling patterns for handling problems in writing and editing papers. Here is a real-life example:

Jonathan had the scare of his life during his freshman year in college. One day after turning in the draft of a writing assignment to his English teacher, he was asked to stay after class. The graduate student who taught the class told him that she was going to have to refer him to the Honor Court for suspected cheating. Jonathan was immediately thrown into a state of panic! The instructor pointed out that there were two handwriting samples on the draft he turned in, and obviously he had gotten more help on the paper than the honor code at college would allow. She could tell that there was another person writing on the paper and changing Jonathan's spelling and grammar throughout the paper. Jonathan explained that because of his learning disability in writing language, his mother had always edited his papers in high school with his special class teacher's blessing. Both Jonathan and his mother were shocked to learn that according to the honor code, this type of help was considered cheating at college. When his case went to the Honor Court, Jonathan was found not guilty, but the stress he and his family endured took its toll on his performance in all of his classes.

While many teens diagnosed with ADHD or LD rely on others to edit their papers, they don't all end up in front of the Honor Court at college. However, many experience a great deal of stress because they have not learned how to independently move through all stages in the writing process to produce their best work. At college, transitioning students meet multiple writing assignments that are longer and much more complex than anything they faced previously. Sometimes, several papers are due during the same week of the semester. Unlike high school, where several smaller writing assignments are given and checked to make sure the student is working on the larger paper, in college the student is on her own.

Facing these new expectations can be overwhelming if a student's disability interferes with any aspect of the writing process, especially if the student received help from parents and teachers who won't be available in college. For example, some students depend on receiving extensions as a way to cope with their writing difficulties. Others, like Jonathan, have asked parents, relatives, friends, or even the teacher to read and help edit their papers. Because assignments tend to be less complex in high school and community college, many students have learned to wait until the deadline and to write one draft of a paper. Many times these patterns have been rewarded with fairly good grades, so students don't see a need to change what they are doing until they are in college.

By choosing to work on this skill now, it is hoped your teen will avoid the undue stress that college-level writing assignments can cause. The following tips may help him develop this skill.

**Pinpoint the problem.** Think about what part of the writing process is hardest and why. Look at old papers and identify patterns in teacher feedback.

**Analyze approach to writing papers.** Does your teen realize that writing is a process that happens over time, or is she used to writing a final product close to the deadline?

**Learn about the writing process.** Encourage your teen to do an Internet search or to take out a library book about the writing process.

**Identify resources.** Identify the available resources at school to work on writing. Is the English teacher available to work one-on-one with your teen on assignments? What about the special class teacher?

**Consider learning styles.** Have your teen think more about his learning style and how this knowledge can be applied to writing. What process would help him to organize and clarify ideas for a paper? Would talking the ideas through with the teacher or a friend help? Would taping the ideas be helpful before actually typing or writing them on the page? Would using a mind map or mind-mapping software like Inspiration (http://www.inspiration.com) help your teen generate ideas and then organize them together?

**Use technology.** Voice recognition software is built into some operating systems or can be purchased by Nuance (http://shop.nuance.com/store/nuanceus/html/pbPage.dns-page1/ThemeID.13735700). It allows a person to talk, and the computer types what is being said. While it isn't foolproof, it can help students who are more verbal, those who have trouble holding on to their ideas long enough to write them, as well as those who find writing or typing to be laborious.

**Develop a proofreading process.** Once again an Internet search can help you and your teen create a process. When proofreading a paper on the computer, you can make the font very large and double space the text. Collapse the window so only a line or two of text shows up at a time. Use the highlighting feature to mark errors or sections of the paper that need to be reworked rather than immediately making revisions. That way, the proofreading step is separated from the writing step. Here are some other general tips for proofreading that you might want to suggest to your teen:

• Take a break after writing and before proofreading a paper.

• Read the paper out loud to hear errors and other problems in the paper.

• Consider using a text-reading software to read the paper back aloud.

**Create a checklist.** Help your teen make a personalized proofreading checklist based on her unique error patterns.

## Preparing For and Taking Tests

Many high school students, even those without disabilities, think they are very good at preparing for tests and exams and are totally shocked to realize that their methods are not going to work in college. The types of tests given at most high schools are not as complex as those your teen will get in college. Tests in high school and even in community colleges tend to occur more frequently and cover smaller amounts of information. In addition, most exams in these settings require students to memorize information such as new vocabulary, facts, concepts, or formulas. However, tests in college tend to expect students to apply the factual knowledge they are learning and to think more critically. Critical thinking is a much more active process and requires the learner to analyze and synthesize information by putting it together to see relationships, similarities, and differences and to form well-supported conclusions. Because many teens, not just those diagnosed with ADHD or LD, have limited experience with this type of thinking, they are frequently unprepared for the exams they face at college.

Because your teen has chosen to work on this skill, you can influence him to become more prepared for taking tests now and in the future. The following tips may help in that process.

**Define strengths and weakness.** Ask about examples when your teen felt that she was well prepared for an exam, especially a final exam covering a lot of information. What strategies were used? What worked and what didn't?

**Analyze different strategies.** Ask about strategies for preparing for different types of exams (multiple choice, short answer, and essay) as well as different subjects (history, science, English, math, etc.). What worked? What didn't work? Sometimes problems happen when a student takes an exam. If your teen has trouble with this skill, check out "Common Test-Taking Strategies" at the end of this chapter for suggestions.

**Create a file of successful strategies.** Create a file of strategies that work for different classes and different test formats. Make sure the file accompanies your teen when he goes off to college.

**Identify resources.** Identify the resources in school and in the community for learning more about how to better prepare for tests and final exams and what books are available in the school or community library. Check out the books listed in the resource section at the end of this guide.

**Conduct an error analysis.** Look at error patterns on old exams to figure out what went wrong. Were questions missed because the questions were not read carefully? Were careless errors made because of rushing and not double checking work?

**Monitor time.** Encourage your teen to think about how to use and monitor time during an exam. If anxiety is an issue during an exam, encourage your teen to search online for strategies to manage anxiety. If anxiety is a major barrier during exams, consider getting some professional help now to avoid bigger problems later on.

## Studying Regularly

This is one skill that few first-year students have practiced, yet it is critical to success in 4-year colleges. Certainly, most high schools have daily graded homework and frequent quizzes and tests that serve the purpose of keeping students up-to-date with work. Similarly, many times students who attend community colleges report that their participation in class is expected given the smaller class size, so they stay on top of work out of necessity. Many even report that they have frequent exams similar to the schedule that they had in high school. As a result most students really don't have any idea of what to do when they are told to study. If there isn't any assigned homework or if a test isn't scheduled, they think they have nothing to do.

This type of thinking usually backfires in colleges where there may be very little assigned, graded outside-of-class work (with the exception of foreign language classes, math, and calculation-based classes). When college students without attention or learning disabilities discover that they have to cram for an exam, they may be more successful because they may still be able to call upon their executive functioning skills under pressure and prioritize, problem-solve, and generally work more quickly. Unfortunately, students diagnosed with ADHD or LD may have much more difficulty being strategic in a crisis when they realize that they have considerable work to do to prepare for a test or complete a paper that is due soon. Instead, their stress and difficulty with self-management can block them from problem-solving and finding a way to tackle the crisis. In addition, their tendency to work more slowly makes it almost impossible for them to handle this challenging situation.

It is great that your teen has chosen to work on this very critical study skill now in order to avoid these later problems. You can help your teen create an action plan for this skill by using the following tips.

**Test it out.** Identify one or two classes in which his performance could be improved by studying regularly. Develop a table with the grades from previous tests and quizzes to compare with those taken after your teen begins studying more.

**Create a personalized plan.** Perhaps this plan could include daily study sessions in addition to time set aside to complete homework. If your teen has trouble with studying regularly, check out "Plan for Study Sessions" at the end of the chapter for suggestions.

## Seeking Out Tutors and Extra Help When Needed

For many of the study skills listed in this chapter, we suggest that you help your teen identify all the available resources. We believe quite strongly that successful students use resources. In fact, we believe that successful people use resources. Yet we see many college students, even those without disabilities, who have not developed this skill. Too often, we encounter students who feel that using a resource, like tutoring or a learning or writing center, is a sign of weakness. They seem to think that they should be able to figure everything out on their own because they have in the past. The truth is that for many students, even those with disabilities, this has been the case. They have been successful pretty much on their own by just trying harder and putting in the necessary time. Thus, they may have no experience with going to a tutor or a learning specialist. Those students who struggled when younger, received special services, and used tutors and teachers may actually have a "leg up" because they have already learned that it is acceptable and even valuable to reach out for help. Some students with attention and learning challenges may have learned to ask their parents or siblings for help. Either their shyness or their feelings of shame have led them to seek help within the safety of their family. However, while these students may have gotten good grades as a result, they also are not experienced at going to strangers and getting the academic help they need.

To help your teen work on this skill during high school, have him try some or all of the following tips.

**Research the range of academic help available at school.** Suggest using the school website and talking to the guidance counselor or special class teacher to get a full picture of all the academic help available.

**Form a study group.** Talk with friends to see if any of them might be interested in forming a study group. This is what many successful college students do.

> ➡ **Coaching Reminder!** Going to help sessions pre-
> pared makes it easier. Help your teen prepare by making
> a list of questions and maybe even practicing what to
> say when she is confused. Speaking up like this can be
> hard at first, especially if your teen is shy and new to get-
> ting help. She may even want to role play this with you.
> If remembering what is said at the help session is as much
> a weakness for your teen as taking notes, then encourage
> her to ask permission to tape the session using a digital
> recorder or the Livescribe Pen.

## Skill: Time Management

One of the first issues your teen will have to face after you unpack the car, leave him in the dorm, and wave goodbye is what to do with all that unstructured time. When will he study? How much downtime should he have for socializing and other activities? When will he work on long-term assignments and projects? If your teen has never had to make a decision about when and what to do, this new experience may be overwhelming. It's extremely important that both you and your teen acknowledge now that this skill needs to be worked on before college. Because so many parents play an enabling role in how their teen manages time, we have a number of suggestions for you as well as for your teen. Let's get started on how to hand over the controls to your teen for managing time.

### Setting Up Study Schedules for Homework and Other Assignments

First, think about the role you currently play in helping your teen stick to a study schedule. Are you being an enabler? Try observing yourself for a few days or a week and keeping track of what you are saying and doing to help create and enforce your teen's study schedule. Are you always the one setting rules about when to do homework and making sure the electronic equipment in the house is off? Are you constantly reminding your teen about the family's weekend plans in advance so she knows that Saturday afternoon is the best time to work on the science report? Are you playing a more hidden role by walking in and out of her bedroom to see what she is doing?

If your teen has lots of time before college, you might begin to work on moving him toward independence in this area by meeting once a week and looking over the upcoming assignments and big projects. Then, using your best coaching skills, ask questions to guide him to set up a plan for studying and completing all of his work on time. Ask what role your teen wants you to play as he follows the plan. Be sure to state what your limits are. And be very clear about the enabling roles you are no longer willing to play.

If there isn't much time left to practice before college and you are going cold turkey, talk with your teen to discuss ideas for setting up a schedule and ask what role she would like you to play for support, and then let go. Yes, it is scary. Your teen could choose to put other interests and activities above work and her grades may suffer. But isn't it better for her to learn this now with you around to help her learn from her mistakes?

Remember to set up a time to talk to evaluate the plan. You can ask some great coaching questions that promote growth and responsibility in this area. Remember that soon enough you won't be able to provide any input on when your teen chooses to study, and that by allowing him to make mistakes now, you may be preventing even bigger problems at college.

## Tackling Daily Homework

Tackling daily homework can be extremely challenging for teens diagnosed with ADHD or LD. For some, this type of work may be impossible because of all the obstacles created by their organizational difficulties; for others, it is a time-management issue. Even though college classes rarely have daily, graded homework, some classes do require daily practice to learn skills that build on one another. Being able to consistently complete daily assignments in high school can set the stage for learning to do all the practice work that is required at college.

Since your teen has rated this skill as one that needs to be worked on, you can help her develop the ability to do work on a more consistent basis that will be important in college. The following tips can help you and your teen develop this important skill.

**Map it out.** Many books on time management suggest that the first step is to map out an hour-by-hour master schedule of the week to raise awareness of how much time is available and then to highlight the open, unstructured times.

**Have a system.** Encourage your teen to think about what system he wants to use to map out and look at what blocks of time are available. Would using a paper calendar work for this purpose? Would an online calendar, like Google calendar (http://www.google.com/googlecalendar/about.html) be of interest? Or does your teen have a cell phone with a calendar system to lay out a schedule? Would your teen prefer to use a large desk memo calendar or a big white board where he can write his plan and not avoid seeing it? Would your teen want to use small post-it notes to write up plans for each day? Remember, there is no correct way. Help your teen be creative and experiment until he finds a method that works!

**Plug in homework and long-term assignments.** Once the master calendar is completed, encourage your teen to look at where there is some unstructured time in her life. It might be interesting to actually count the hours available each day. Then encourage her to think about what activities or tasks, like homework or working on long-term assignments, might best fit into these open blocks of time.

**Improve motivation.** If the problem is attitude or motivation, encourage your teen to talk to friends, siblings, or cousins who are already in college, and ask them about the importance of doing daily work. Encourage your teen to come up with a reason that doing daily homework is important to him and then write up a "pep talk" on a note card that can be posted somewhere prominent.

**Find the best time.** Encourage your teen to think about when is the best time during the day to get daily homework and special assignments done. Is there time in school during study hall? Would it work out for your teen to stay after school and do homework where tutoring sessions are held, just in case questions arise? Or would your teen be motivated to go to the community library or a local coffee shop to do daily home-work right after school? Doing homework before coming home can prevent the organizational problems some teens have and can also give a sense of being done with school work once she arrives home. This habit may serve your teen well in college.

## Dealing With Long-Term Assignments and Keeping Track of Important Due Dates

Many college students, not just those with ADHD or LD, have to spend the first semester at college figuring out what system will work for them. These students experience stress when they discover that the due dates are not predictable and that college professors don't give a lot of reminders. Instead, professors expect the students to go to the class website and know when tests and papers are due. Students often have difficulty with this new system, and they typically discover that they can't keep all this information in their heads like they did in high school.

In addition, there are lots of other important dates college students need to know, including the deadline for adding and dropping classes, paying tuition bills, registering for the next semester, requesting accommodations, meeting with advisers, selecting a major, studying abroad, applying for scholarships, requesting dorm room assignments, and buying tickets to sporting or social events. The list goes on and on. These important dates may be communicated once, via e-mail, and unless a teen has a system to keep track of these dates, opportunities will be lost.

It is hoped that by using the tips above and creating a plan and master schedule, your teen will be able to manage and deal with the first semester of college and this new style of assigning tasks more successfully. If they do mess up, it's better that it happen in high school where they typically can learn from their mistakes without significant academic, emotional, and financial consequences.

# COMMON TEST-TAKING STRATEGIES

1. Spread studying out over time, because it is not easy for anyone, even those without disabilities, to review and remember too much information in one sitting.

2. Be sure about what the test will cover and how the teacher will expect you to show what you know.

3. Start by studying the information that is less familiar and ending with the information that just needs to be reviewed. If time runs short, studying the harder information first will pay off.

4. Make up questions as a way to test your knowledge for the exam.

5. Look at old exams and study guides and then create sample test questions.

6. Look at the back of the book for questions, especially those that require you to apply or critically use the information.

7. Use the syllabus and course objectives to create a study guide and sample questions.

8. Practice the type of thinking that college tests will require, and go beyond the fact level of who, what, when, and where. Practice comparing and contrasting information. Practice describing and giving examples. Practice identifying the significance of a person, event, or place. For science classes, practice explaining the function of an organ, compare and contrast different plants or animals, or describe the structure of an organ. For math and calculation-based classes, practice doing problems without opening the book. If the test is an essay, practice writing an essay.

# PLAN FOR STUDY SESSIONS

1.  Reread class notes and summarize the key concepts and ideas taught in the class.

2.  Create sample test questions on this material and practice answering the questions.

3.  Consult other sources on the same subject to study the information. Is there another book on the subject that could be read or any information that is available on the Internet?

4.  Create study guides that match your learning style. Would it be helpful to study with a friend and practice teaching each other? Would it help to tape record a summary of the information studied? Would a written summary be better? What about creating a visual of the information, like a flow chart, table, or graph?

# Chapter 9
## Proof That a Successful Solo Flight *Is* Possible

Success in college and beyond is possible for young adults who have challenges in how they learn and pay attention. While they may need more deliberate training from adults and much more support to be ready for take-off and during their first solo flight, that doesn't mean they can't develop what it takes to successfully navigate in the new world of college.

In this chapter, you will hear from some actual college students who have "made it" and arrived at their destination. Although they encountered many of the same challenges as the teens you met at the start of this book, they were better equipped to maneuver around the turbulence and storms they encountered. One of the young adults did not receive much preparation for college and experienced a solo flight at a 4-year college that had to be aborted. Despite his unexpected challenges, even this young man shows that it is never too late to get the training and support you need. After learning some very important lessons, he, too, experienced success.

Three of these teens were successful because they were strategically prepared with many of the readiness skills found in this book. While these teens and their parents didn't have the benefit of a complete Personalized College Readiness Program like the one we are offering you here, they were able to piece together some of the components during their time in high school. All three had some specialized preparation designed by their proactive parents. For some, encounters with therapists, special class teachers, coaches, or tutors helped them better understand the nature of their disabilities, better understand what they needed, and practice asking for and receiving help. There was deliberate work on the part of their parents to prepare them to be their own advocates and to have those all-important self-determination, daily living, and study skills in order for them to handle the college environment. These three students were willing, at their parents prompting, to put transition supports in place, either in the form of a summer transition program or immediately connecting with campus and community supports.

## Successful Students

These young adults, as well as their parents, would concur that the journey before and during college has not been a smooth one. Each teen encountered his or her share of challenges, even the three who had spent time planning and preparing before taking off to college. The solo flights for some had to be rerouted. Others had to make emergency landings. One did not have a direct flight to success. But all agree they wouldn't trade their life-changing journeys. These young adults were willing to share their stories, including the downs as well as the ups, so that you and your teen could benefit from what they have learned. More importantly, they want their stories to give you and your teen hope that having a successful transition to college really is possible!

## Meet Emily: A Freshman at a Large State University (With a Transition Program)

Emily was diagnosed in elementary school and received special services for her learning disability in reading, writing, and her predominantly inattentive type of attention-deficit/hyperactivity disorder (ADHD). Additional emotional issues complicated Emily's situation, necessitating the inclusion of a therapist to her team of professionals. Because she is a shy, somewhat anxious young woman, her parents made sure that she began to practice talking to her teachers on her own in high school. They also found some college transition programs to let her slowly practice being independent and advocating for herself while she was still in high school. When Emily was accepted to several large state universities, her parents literally forced her to attend the only one that had a transition program that would allow her to live on campus for an entire summer session before starting her freshman year. They knew that their daughter would benefit from getting this trial practice run.

In spite of all their planning and structuring, Emily still encountered a very rough first year at college. Many of her classes were reading and writing intensive with a number of difficult papers and projects. Even with support from the writing center, Emily was overwhelmed. She also had a social crisis that put her into an emotional tailspin right near the end of the fall semester. In the spring semester, her difficulty asking for help and her time-management struggles caused another crisis. Emily was unable to finish a very long paper that was the only grade in one of her classes. Unable to seek help from the professor due to his more formal demeanor, Emily approached the end the spring semester in another state of panic.

Emily and her parents learned that no matter how much preparation there is, you can't prepare for every possible problem. A total crisis was averted, however, because Emily had practice asking for help and was familiar with all of the key support people on her campus and in the community.

**Emily speaks:** "During the summers before my 11th- and 12th-grade year, I attended two summer programs at a college. Although they weren't at the college I eventually attended, going to these still helped me a lot. I got used to being on my own, and I practiced advocating for myself and setting up my own accommodations. This made it easier for me to practice talking with my teachers on my own during my last couple of years in high school instead of relying on my mother to talk to them for me.

I am surprised that I didn't really have trouble meeting new friends; it hasn't been a big deal like it was in high school. I think that's because of the summer transition program where I just got "clumped" together with the kids there. But it's also been easier meeting other kids, too. I think at college there's a larger variety of people, there aren't the judgments like in high school, and no one knew about my disabilities. But no doubt the summer transition program was very important to my adjustment, even though I wasn't thrilled that my parents made me do it. Without it, I would have been pretty lost when I got here. Instead, I was familiar with my surroundings, had a relationship with my advisor and the Disabilities Services Office, and started working with my coach. During the summer, I took two classes and started the fall with a good GPA. This ended up being really important because I had trouble taking a full course load my first semester and got an Incomplete in one class during my second semester, and those count as Fs until you make up the work.

Setting up my support system in the summer before I started classes was really important. This helped me get to know all the new people at my college and feel comfortable going to them when I needed to. When I met with my advisor during the crisis in the fall, I learned that there was a special procedure to request dropping one class and finishing the fall semester with a temporary underload. In the spring semester, I also turned to my advisor and discovered that I could request an Incomplete from my professor and finish the paper over the summer. While I wish things had gone better, I am proud that I finished my freshman year. I've learned from my mistakes and registered for a better balance of classes for next fall. I plan to work with my campus coach to develop and follow a better study schedule and seek out help much sooner from my professors."

## Meet Cecelia: A Sophomore at a 4-Year College With a Campus Disabilities Services Program

Cecelia has successfully finished her second year at a 4-year college. Like Emily, she was diagnosed in elementary school and knew she needed to immediately connect with the campus's Disabilities Services program. As a matter of fact, she had an appointment the first day classes began during her freshman year. Cecelia's parents did much to prepare her to understand how her reading disability affected her and to know what she needed to do to overcome it. As a result, she came to college with a host of study skills to compensate for her struggles in reading. However, no one predicted how underdeveloped her self-advocacy skills were and how hard it would be, given her slow-to-adjust nature, to make friends and feel connected socially on a large campus.

**Cecelia speaks:** "The switch from a small school where I never had more than 25 students in a class to a large college where my smallest classes had a minimum of 100 students was really tough. I had such close relationships with my teachers in high school that I never had to ask for help or to explain my disability. Everyone in my school knew about my dyslexia and my teachers would notice if I was struggling and help me out. College took self-advocating to a whole new level. It was the first time I had to make the effort to get to know my teachers and get the help I needed. Because I knew I needed help for my learning disabilities, I scheduled weekly meetings with a learning specialist right away. So, thankfully, I had the support I needed to do a crash course in how to be proactive and talk to my professors. My learning specialist understood the way I felt about going to office hours and helped me practice what to say so I could quickly get over my shyness about meeting with them. She encouraged me to use the letter that the Disabilities Services Office sent out as an "ice breaker" and follow this up with my own personal e-mail explaining my disability and asking to set up a meeting time. We actually role played the meetings and this really helped.

For some reason, I also had this fantasy that it would be really easy for me to get involved at college and make friends. I always imagined that I would join some clubs and, just like that, I would make new best friends. But I didn't really realize how shy I can be until I get used to a new place. I only had one big transition before college when I left elementary school and moved to the next school where I attended middle and high school all in the same building. I totally forgot about how hard that adjustment was and how much teasing I got for having to attend a special education class. The same feelings of fear and insecurity that shut me down then haunted me at college. I panicked when I thought about joining clubs or intramural sports activities where there wouldn't be anyone I knew. Although I had some friends from high school who came to my college, I didn't live in the same dorms they did and didn't want to pledge a sorority right away like they did. I knew that the adjustment to the classes would be really hard for me at first because of my reading and writing problems, and I couldn't handle all the time that pledging would take up. So, I was really lost, felt lonely, and I hadn't expected to feel this way.

During my weekly meetings with my learning specialist, we spent part of the time brainstorming strategies to help me develop a social support network in a way that better matched my personality. I learned to use the friends I knew from high school as my home base, making sure that I met up with one of them every day for lunch, dinner, or study time. Then things kind of branched out from there, and I met the friends they met, and soon I had a bigger network of people I knew. By my second year of college I had the courage to branch out on my own and join some groups and clubs that matched my interests and I didn't need the weekly meetings with my learning specialist. I'm feeling brave now and have signed up to spend my junior year studying abroad in France. Who would have believed that I would even consider such a big step?"

## Meet Spencer: A Junior at a 4-Year College

Spencer was also diagnosed in elementary school with a disability that interfered with his ability to read and spell words, memorize details, and to learn a foreign language. He always excelled in the sciences and math-based classes and he needed very little help prior to college. He did great as long as teachers didn't count off for his spelling errors on tests and if he could use spell check on the computer when he wrote papers and took essay exams. His high school had waived its foreign language requirement for him, and he was shocked to learn that this did not automatically happen at his college.

Spencer's mom, who was a single parent, needed him to carry his part of the load in their day-to-day life. He therefore came to college with a toolbox full of daily living skills. In fact, Spencer brags about the fact that he was the one in his freshman dorm who taught everyone how to do the laundry and how to open a bank account and use an ATM card. Because of his mother's busy work schedule, he spent summers away from home visiting relatives out of state and attending camps, so he had no trouble adjusting to being on his own and forming close friendships and joining organizations. He didn't need to develop many study skills because of how bright he was and the less demanding academic expectations he had experienced in high school. However, he still managed to get fairly good grades.

Because he always had some accommodations throughout school, he was open to registering with the Disabilities Services Office on campus; and, like Emily and Cecelia, he wanted to play it safe during his first semester, so he quickly set up weekly appointments with a learning specialist. He had no problem talking with his professors, explaining his disability and talking about his accommodations. His great organizational and time-management skills allowed him to keep track of all of his tests and assignments and to schedule his testing accommodations. Overall, he had an excellent adjustment to being on his own.

However, his first major challenge came almost immediately when he learned that the college wouldn't honor his foreign language waiver. Although he was stressed about it, he registered for Swahili because it didn't rely on phonics like the romance languages did. Spencer made sure he still had weekly meetings with his learning specialist. He had to quickly swallow his pride and attend tutoring sessions, hoping these would help him learn a foreign language. To his surprise, he passed the class and was able to move on to the next level of Swahili.

While his first year ended fairly well, it wasn't until his second year that things really came to a head. No one predicted that the same difficulties recalling details that contributed to his problems with spelling and learning a foreign language would also show up in his science major. Spencer dreamed of being a pharmacist and majored in chemistry assuming that he would excel in it like he did in high school. However, his disabilities made it nearly impossible for him to write formulas correctly on the challenging tests he faced in these classes. This crisis stopped Spencer dead in his tracks, and he had to find a new route to follow to get his degree and reach his goal of pharmacy school.

**Spencer speaks:** "The tests in my upper-level chemistry classes were unlike anything I had in high school. I didn't have a clue about what they would be like and I was studying like I always had. Because the first tests didn't occur for almost 6 weeks, I was blown away by how ridiculously hard they were. They weren't multiple-choice exams, so I had to actually write out the formulas and apply them to different types of problems. I encountered real difficulty when I tried to memorize all the details of the formulas. So, I got much lower grades than I ever had before and I was devastated. I immediately realized that my whole approach to studying had to change. I needed to get help from tutors, something I never had to do before. With help from my learning specialist, I also had to rethink how much time I had to spend studying and really figure out what strategies might work better for me to memorize formulas.

But nothing seemed to work. I came face-to-face with the truth that my learning disabilities were real and I might have to give up my dream. I dropped my upper-level chemistry class and decided to take it in summer school, thinking that if it was the only class I had, I could give it all the time I needed. But, when I took it again, I had the same problems. Nothing I did helped! I couldn't hold all the details of the formulas in my head. I talked to the professor to see if they would let me have multiple-choice tests, but the answer was 'no'. I dropped the summer school course and went home for the rest of the summer feeling defeated. For the first time in my life, I couldn't overcome a problem. I felt horrible and became depressed, angry, and frustrated. For a good 6 months, I struggled with the realization that my dreams might not be possible; I may have picked the wrong major given my learning disabilities. While my mother tried to be encouraging and my learning specialist did her best, no one could help me. A part of me wanted to run away and avoid it all, another part of me helped me realize that I had to redefine what success meant and see that I had options. I could transfer to an easier school, totally give up my dream of pharmacy school, or even change my major. One day, I just said to myself, 'You can feel anyway you want, but you have to decide on what action to take.' I learned from my academic advisor that I could take this same upper-level chemistry course somewhere else where the tests might not require me to recall the information. This new idea opened my mind to other possibilities. I researched how the college near my home taught this class. I learned that the tests there were multiple choice. I worked with the admissions office to make sure the course I took at home transferred back to my college and that it would count toward my major. So, I took this course in summer school near my home and got an A.

This year I decided to go for it and applied to several pharmacy programs knowing that I might not get accepted. When I was home for winter break, I learned that I had been accepted into my top choice program. I plan to give it a try knowing that it may or may not work out. The struggles I went through taught me so much about myself. Now, I know more about my strengths and my weaknesses. Most important, I know that there are always options, even when you don't think there are!"

## Meet Ethan: A Transfer Student From a Community College

Unlike all the other students you have met, Ethan didn't come to college fully understanding his ADHD, and he didn't start out connected to any resources. His path to a 4-year college was also different, starting first at a local community college and then transferring to the state college of his dreams. While his ADHD had always led him to be a slow reader, a bit disorganized, fidgety, and inattentive, none of these issues led to major problems for him before. Ethan had innate intelligence, determination, and a charismatic personality. All these strengths allowed him to be successful in the smaller, interactive classes in high school and community college where he didn't have to seek out formal accommodations. He could avoid reading the assignments by listening carefully in class and going to meet with teachers and professors individually to get a verbal explanation if he was confused. When he ran out of time on tests or needed more time for a project or paper, this assertive, personable young man discovered that he could ask for flexibility and usually things went his way. He was a leader in high school and at his community college and had always lived a full life. Although he had been very successful at the community college, he did not feel challenged and he looked forward to being at the more prestigious and competitive 4-year college.

But as the old proverb says, "Be careful what you wish for, you just might get it," Ethan got his wish along with the greatest challenges he had ever faced in his life. As a transfer student, he was placed in higher level classes in his major based on the assumption that he had adequate preparation from the classes he took at the community college. Instantly, Ethan experienced what is referred to in the research as "transfer shock," when a transfer student transitions to a new, more demanding, larger university and becomes insecure and overwhelmed. Also as a first-generation college student who had never experienced failure and on whom so many family members were counting, he hesitated to tell his parents what was really happening. However, he had connected with the transfer student supports on campus and had a close mentor in the first-generation program to whom he turned.

**Ethan speaks:** "Transferring to this college has been the most difficult experience of my life! Immediately, I felt lost on campus and lost in my large lecture classes. I was overwhelmed by how fast things moved in the classes and the fact that there weren't many small group opportunities to use my approach of asking questions to make up for what I couldn't get from the readings. Instantly, I felt stupid, like I didn't belong here and that everyone else was smarter than me. While I knew I had ADHD, I had never needed medication or any support to be successful. In fact, I viewed getting any help—medication, study skills help, tutoring, or accommodations—as a sign of weakness, crutches that I didn't want to rely on.

I realized that I didn't have the study skills needed in this new type of learning environment where I had to read tons of pages each day and figure out a lot on my own. I didn't feel like I could go talk to my professors because they seemed so different from the teachers I had in high school and the instructors at the community college. When I failed my first midterm exams in most of my classes, I did have the good sense to talk to the first-generation mentor. He clued me in on the campus Learning Center where I could get some help with study skills. However, the help I got was 'too little, too late' and I couldn't pull my grades up. I was placed on probation, which gave me one semester to get my grades back to where they needed to be so that I could remain in good standing. However, with an even crazier spring schedule and still refusing to get help, things only got worse! I got more and more depressed, and eventually

I had to tell my parents that the first kid in our family who went off to college was failing miserably. They were so supportive, but it didn't take away my shame. After talking with a counselor on campus and my first-generation mentor, we decided that I needed to withdraw.

I guess sometimes you really do have to 'hit bottom' for things to get better. It was at the lowest point in my life when my first-generation mentor confronted me about the fact that I really needed to consider medication, registering for accommodations, and continuing to use the Learning Center when I returned. The counselor at the Counseling Center also told me that I would need to get therapy for my depression and have proof of my progress in writing from my therapist before I could return to campus. I hated these suggestions and didn't want to hear them. Getting help seemed so negative to me. When I talked to my parents, they were totally in agreement and encouraged me to get the help I needed so that I could be successful when I returned to college.

And, as hard as it was, it actually was helpful to face that I do have a disability. When I returned to college I got started working with a learning specialist, went on the appropriate medication, and accepted accommodations. My old self returned as my life began to turn around. I am graduating this spring and have a job that I am looking forward to. Who knows, I might even consider graduate school in the future. Now I know that I can survive anything and have a lot of hope for my future."

## Why Were These Students Successful?

All of these amazing young adults experienced significant

learning, attention, and emotional challenges during their solo flight to college, even the three students whose parents worked so hard to prepare them. Yet, they all were able to continue and, hopefully, will eventually reach their final destination: graduation! It is important to note, however, that we have also met students who we believe are success stories even though they haven't graduated and discovered that college wasn't for them. Even if students choose instead to follow a passion like acting or to find a career that they find fulfilling, this is something to celebrate. We have also met students whose solo flights were much longer, as they had some side journeys away from college to work or to find themselves and then came back many years later and finished. We have also met some who found success after finishing a 2-year degree or enlisted in the Army and stopped there.

We do realize, however, that many teens and families do define success as getting a 4-year degree. So, we believe we can learn a lot from these young adults who did make it and think about their "secrets to success." These students had some qualities that allowed them to avoid a total disaster. All of these students had the following strategies in common.

**Sought out and accepted support.** It is important to note that the three students who didn't try to go it alone had the support they needed when crises hit. So many times, students who know they have unique needs want to leave their problems in high school and hope that these differences will magically no longer cause them difficulties. Unfortunately, these students tend to do this at one of the most challenging transitions in their lives. Sometimes, bright successful students with disabilities like Ethan can get far with informal help and don't really hit the wall until they are at a 4-year college and the expectations escalate. However, Emily, Cecelia, and Spencer each knew, from their past experiences, that they were going to need support as they transitioned. By connecting with the Disabilities Services program on campus and other resources, they were at a distinct advantage at handling the unexpected turbulence that cropped up during their solo flights. This connection not only offered them support and a home base but also allowed them to find out what options were available on campus for the challenges they encountered. Ethan, after hitting bottom, was eventually receptive to seeking out and using resources, and his situation improved dramatically. So, in our opinion, being able to seek out and use resources is a key quality for your teen to develop that may act as a preventative measure against being totally forced off course while learning to navigate all the challenges that your teen will most definitely encounter in college.

**Honestly faced their struggles.** Similarly, all four students were able to honestly accept and admit their struggles, first to themselves and then to someone else, even if not to their parents. So often when teens encounter their "first failure" experiences, they tend to feel shame and embarrassment, like Ethan did, which prevents them for letting anyone know. In each case, these teens had a relationship with some trusted adult, either at the Disabilities Services program or some other program on or off campus with whom they were honest about their struggles. Most colleges have special procedures for various crises, like when Emily had an emotional crisis and could not finish the semester with a full course load, when Ethan needed to withdraw due to depression, or when Spencer was unable to pass a required course in his major. However, unless a teen is honest about his or her struggles and lets someone know the truth, wheels cannot be put into motion to implement the procedures that do exist for such unique circumstances. Frequently, when students don't share their struggles and crises, they tend to assume that there are no solutions and that their situation is hopeless.

**Adapted to their new setting.** Although all of the teens in this chapter met challenges, they all eventually adapted to the situations they encountered. Emily had to accept the fact that her parents gave her no choice in which college to attend and went off to a summer transition program the day after her high school graduation. Cecelia had to find ways to deal with the fact that she knew very few people on her new campus and that she had to be proactive about talking with her professors. She had to be flexible and do some things that weren't easy for her to do. Spencer had to accept going to tutors, something he had never done, to pass Swahili. Ethan had to accept the reality that he couldn't ignore his disability and accept medical treatment and accommodations.

**Persisted, even when there was little evidence that things could get better.** Persisting, even when things were bleak, was a quality that all of these teens had in common. Because of the supports they were using and the relationships they formed, these teens were helped to take the steps to continue navigating through very stormy times. Their desire not to quit, their dreams of graduation, and their goals for the future allowed each of them to stay the course. Even Ethan, who had to leave college for a period of time, did what it took to get back and take control of his life again.

**Learned from their mistakes and struggles.** Finally, all of these teens used the challenges they experienced during their solo flights as learning experiences and worked to adopt new attitudes and behaviors that led to their eventual success. They all uniformly agree that they are still glad they came to college and faced the reality. They are all stronger and wiser as a result.

## Final Words of Advice

The final words of advice for you and your teen came from Ethan, who had struggled and hit bottom before getting the help he needed and who turned his life around: "I think the absolutely most important thing teens need to know is never give up and always know that despite whatever struggles or problems they may have, there is a solution or someone who can help them, even when they feel things are hopeless. I hope they can also avoid some of the problems I had. I'd encourage them to find out how different and difficult being in a 4-year college really is before they get there and get ready now! I wish my parents and I would have had a book like this one to use. Maybe I would have had an easier time figuring it all out."

## Conclusion: When It's Time for Take-Off

We know that you are just finishing this book and that it will take some time for you to learn how to coach your teen and for the two of you to design and implement your teen's Personalized College Readiness Program. We realize that you still have a lot of hard work ahead of you. However, when you have used what you are learning in this guide for some time, your teen will become more prepared and you will become more of an expert at all the skills and steps provided in this guide. And soon, when all the hard work and planning is over, it will be time for your teen to take off and to begin to fly solo.

When this time comes, there will be a new role for you to play. A role that may, indeed, be a tough one for you to get used to and equally challenging for your teen. As the stories of the teens in this chapter demonstrate, most solo flights will inevitably encounter some turbulence and maybe even some stormy conditions. But you have a greater awareness and many skills that will ensure that you are empowering your transitioning college student to take the controls on this important journey. Also, know that your teen will grow, become more familiar with how to maneuver through these unfamiliar conditions, and find the way in this new territory. Throughout your son's or daughter's life, you have learned that challenges and, yes, even failures, can be valuable opportunities for your teen to become confident, and even more skilled in flying solo.

Be sure to recognize that although your role is changing, you will never stop being a parent! As you design your new role and perfect this new way of communicating, know that although you have left the cockpit, you will always be available remotely from miles away with your cell phone, e-mail, texting, and weekend visits to help your teen get back on course. You and your teen can and will utilize all the skills that you both worked on in the Personalized College Readiness Program that certified him or her to take over the controls.

# References

Barkley, R. A., Murphy, K. R., & Fischer, M. (2007). Adults with ADHD: Clinic-referred cases vs. children grown up. *ADHD Report, 15*(5), 1–7, 13.

Cortiella, C. (2009, June 8). *The state of learning disabilities.* New York, NY: National Center for Learning Disabilities. Retrieved from http://www.ncld.org/stateofld

DeBerard, M. S., Spielmans, G. I., & Julka, D. L. (2004). Predictors of academic achievement and retention among college freshmen: A longitudinal study. *College Student Journal, 38,* 66–80.

Field, S., Martin, J., Miller, R., Ward, M., & Wehmeyer, M. (1998). *A practical guide for teaching self-determination.* Arlington, VA: Council for Exceptional Children.

Gerber, P. J., Reiff, H. B., & Ginsberg, P. (1996). Reframing the learning disabilities experience. *Journal of Learning Disabilities, 29,* 98–101

Heiligenstein, E., Guenther, G., Levey, A., Savino, F., & Fulwiler, J. (1999). Psychological and academic functioning in college students with attention deficit hyperactivity disorder. *Journal of American College Health, 47,* 181–185

Henderson, C. (2001). *College freshmen with disabilities: A biennial statistical profile by the Heath Resource Center* (No. NOH326H98002). Washington, DC: American Council on Education.

Horn, L., & Berktold, J. (1999). *Postsecondary education descriptive analysis reports: Students with disabilities in postsecondary education: A profile of preparation, participation, and outcomes* (Statistical analysis report NCES 1999-187). Washington, DC: U.S. Department of Education.

Jorgensen, S., Fichten, C., & Havel, A. (2003, Spring). *Students with disabilities at Dawson College: Success and outcomes* (Final report). Retrieved from http://adaptech.dawsoncollege.qc.ca/cfichten/PAREA_2k3.pdf

Kuh, G., Kinzie, J., Schuh, J., Whitt, E., & Associates. (2005). *Student success in college: Creating conditions that matter.* San Francisco, CA: Jossey-Bass.

Mattson, C. E. (2007). Beyond admission: Understanding pre-college variables and the success of at-risk students. *Journal of College Admissions, 196,* 8–13.

Murray, C., Goldstein, D., Nourse, S., & Edgar, E. (2000). The postsecondary school attendance and completion rates of high school graduates with LD. *Learning Disabilities Research and Practice, 15,* 119–127.

National Center for Education Statistics. (2000). *Postsecondary students with disabilities: Enrollment, services and persistence* (NCES 2000-092). Washington, DC: U.S. Department of Education. Retrieved from http://nces.ed.gov/pubs2000/2000092.pdf

National Center for Education Statistics. (2002). *Descriptive summary of 1995–96 beginning postsecondary students: Six years later* (NCES 2003-151). Washington, DC: U.S. Department of Education. Retrieved from http://nces.ed.gov/pubsearch/pubsinfo.asp?pubid=2003151.

National Center on Secondary Education and Transition. (2002, March). *Parenting postsecondary students with disabilities: Becoming the mentor, advocate, and guide your young adult needs.* Retrieved from http://www.ncset.org/publications/parent/NCSETParent_Mar02.pdf

National Center for Education Statistics. (2003). *CD-ROM: Beginning postsecondary students longitudinal study: Second follow-up Data Analysis System (DAS) BPS:96/01* (Tables on degree attainment and persistence of 1995–96 beginning post-secondary students in 2001 by disability status and learning disability status). Washington, DC: U.S. Department of Education. Retrieved from http://nces.ed.gov/pubsearch/pubsinfo. asp?pubid=2003159

Newman, L., Wagner, M., Cameto, R., & Knokey, A. M. (2009). *The post-high school outcomes of youth with disabilities up to 4 years after high school: A report from the National Longitudinal Transition Study–2 (NLTS2)* (NCSER 2009-3017). Retrieved from http://www. nlts2.org/reports/2009_04/nlts2_report_2009_04_complete.pdf

Pritchard, M. E., & Wilson, G. S. (2003). Using emotional and social factors to predict student success. *Journal of College Student Development, 44,* 18–28.

Rabiner, D., Anastopoulos, A., Costello, J., Hoyle, R., & Swartzwelder, H. (2008). Adjustment to college in students with ADHD. *Journal of Attention Disorders, 11,* 689–699.

Ridgell, S. D., & Lounsbury, J. W. (2004). Predicting academic success: General intelligence, "Big Five" personality traits, and work drive. *College Student Journal, 38,* 607–618.

Rose, J. (2006). *SMART goal setting: Using the SMART goal setting process to ensure goals are specific.* Retrieved from http://trainingpd.suite101.com/article.cfm/smart_goal_setting

Snyder, T. D., & Hoffman, C. M. (2003). *Digest of education statistics 2002* (NCES 2003-060). Washington, DC: U.S. Government Printing Office. Retrieved from http://nces.ed.gov/ pubsearch/pubsinfo.asp?pubid=2003060

Tinto, V. (1993). *Leaving college: Rethinking the causes and cures of student attrition.* Chicago, IL: University of Chicago Press.

Vogel, S., & Adelman, P. (1990a). Extrinsic and intrinsic factors in graduation and academic failure among LD college students. *Annals of Dyslexia (Orton Dyslexia Society), 40,* 119–137.

Vogel, S., & Adelman, P. (1990b). Intervention effectiveness at the postsecondary level for the learning disabled. In T. Scruggs & B. Wong (Eds.), *Intervention research in learning disabilities* (pp. 329–344). New York, NY: Springer-Verlag.

Vogel, S., & Adelman, P. (2000). Adults with learning disabilities 8–15 years after college. *Learning Disabilities: A Multidisciplinary Journal, 10,* 165–182.

Vogel, S., Leonard, F., Scales, W., Hayeslip, P., Hermansen, J., & Donnells, L. (1998). The national learning disabilities postsecondary data bank: An overview. *Journal of Learning Disabilities, 31,* 234–247.

Vogel, S., Leyser, Y., Wyland, S., & Brulle, A. (1999). Students with learning disabilities in higher education: Faculty attitudes and practices. *Learning Disabilities Research & Practice, 14,* 173–186.

Wagner, M., Newman, L., Cameto, R., Garza, N., & Levine, P. (2005). *After high school: A first look at the postschool experiences of youth with disabilities: A report from the National Longitudinal Transition Study–2 (NLTS2).* Retrieved from http://www.eric.ed.gov/PDFS/ED494935.pdf

Wehmeyer, M. L., & Field, S. L. (2007). *Self determination: Instructional and assessment strategies.* Thousand Oaks, CA: Corwin Press.

# Resource Guide

## Additional Reading for Parents and Educators

Beattie, M. (1987). *Codependent no more: How to stop controlling others and start caring for yourself.* Center City, MN: Hazelden.

Beattie, M. (1989). *Beyond codependency: And getting better all the time.* San Francisco, CA: Harper & Row.

Beattie, M. (2009). *The new codependency: Help and guidance for today's generation.* New York, NY: Simon & Schuster.

Bottke, A. (2008). *Setting boundaries with your adult children.* Eugene, OR: Harvest House.

Conzemius, A., & O'Neill, J. (2001). *The power of SMART goals: Using goals to improve student learning.* Bloomington, IN: Solution Tree Press.

Dawson, J. (2009). *Self-advocacy: A valuable skill for your teenager with LD.* Retrieved from http://www.ldonline.org/article/Self-Advocacy:_A_Valuable_Skill_for_Your_Teenager_with_LD

Fleming, N. (2010). *Vark: A guide to learning styles.* Retrieved from http://www.vark-learn.com

Goldhammer, R., & Brinkerhoff, L. (1993). *Self-advocacy for college students.* Retrieved from http://www.ldonline.org/article/6142

Hazelden/Johnson Institute. (Producer). (1997). *Parenting for prevention: How to stop enabling and start empowering kids.* Minneapolis, MN: Johnson Institute.

Johnson, H., & Schelas-Miller, C. (2000). *Don't tell me what to do, just send money: The essential parenting guide to the college years.* New York, NY: St. Martin's Griffin.

Kiersey Temperament Sorter. (n.d.). Retrieved from http://www.keirsey.com/sorter/instruments2.aspx?partid

Kravitz, M., & Wax, I. (2003). *The K & W guide to colleges for students with learning disabilities and attention deficit disorders: A resource book for students, parents, and professionals* (7th ed.). New York, NY: Princeton Review.

Lowe, K. (2010). *Exercise and ADHD symptoms: How to improve ADHD symptoms with exercise.* Retrieved from http://add.about.com/od/treatmentoptions/a/ratey.htm

Mangrum, C. T., & Strichart, S. (2003). *Peterson's colleges with programs for students with learning disabilities or attention deficit disorders* (7th ed.). Princeton, NJ: Peterson's.

Quinn, P., Ratey, N., & Maitland, T. (2000). *Coaching college students with AD/HD: Issues and answers.* Washington, DC: Advantage Books.

Ratey, J. J., with Hagerman, E. (2008). *Spark: The revolutionary new science of exercise and the brain.* New York, NY: Little Brown.

Solomon, B. A., & Felder, R. M. (n.d.). *Index of Learning Styles Questionnaire.* Raleigh, NC: North Carolina State University. Retrieved from http://www.engr.ncsu.edu/learningstyles/ilsweb.html

*Temperament and change.* (n.d.). Retrieved from http://www.4temperaments.com/change.html

U.S. Department of Education, Office of Civil Rights. (2007, March 16). *Dear parent letter.* Retrieved from http://www2.ed.gov/about/offices/list/ocr/letters/parent-20070316.html

U.S. Department of Education, Office of Civil Rights. (2007, March). *Transition of students with disabilities to postsecondary education: A guide for high school educators.* Retrieved from http://www2.ed.gov/about/offices/list/ocr/transitionguide.html

U.S. Government Accountability Office. (2009, October). *Higher education and disability* (GAO-10-33). Retrieved from http://www.gao.gov/new.items/d1033.pdf

Whitworth, L., Kimsey-House, K., Kimsey-House, H., & Sandahl, P. (2007). *Co-active coaching: New skills for coaching people toward success in work and life* (2nd ed.). Mountain View, CA: Davies-Black.

West, L., Corbey, S., Boyer-Stephens, A., & Jones, B. (1999). *Transition and self-advocacy.* Retrieved from http://www.ldonline.org/article/7757

## Additional Readings for Teens

Bachel, B. (2001). *What do you really want? How to set a goal and go for it! A guide for teens.* Minneapolis, MN: Free Spirit.

*Beat the freshman 15.* (2003, August 2). Retrieved from http://www.ecampustours.com/campuslife/yourfreshmanyear/beat-thefreshman15.htm

Chang, R. (2000). *The passion plan: A step-by-step guide to discovering, developing and living your passion.* San Francisco, CA: Jossey-Bass.

Covey, S. (1998). *The 7 habits of highly effective teens.* New York, NY: Franklin Covery.

Doerflinger, L. (2009, January 21). *Anger management for teens: Self help steps to control your emotions.* Retrieved from http://www.associatedcontent.com/article/1407294/anger_management_for_teens_self_help_pg2.html?cat=72

*Food and fitness resources for teens.* (n.d.). Retrieved from http://kidshealth.org/teen/food_fitness/

Hopkins, L. (2009). *6 tips for effective use of assertive communication.* Retrieved from http://ezinearticles.com/?Assertive-Communication---6-Tips-For-Effective-Use&id=10259

*How can I deal with my anger?* (n.d.). Retrieved from http://kidshealth.org/teen/your_mind/emotions/deal_with_anger.html#

Mooney, J., & Cole, D. (2000). *Learning outside the lines.* New York, NY: Fireside.

Nist, S. L., & Holschuh, J. (2000). *Active learning: Strategies for college success.* Needham Heights, MA: Allyn & Bacon.

Paulk, W., & Owens, R. J. Q. (2007). *How to study in college* (10th ed.). Boston, MA: Houghton Mifflin. Free download: http://the-manuals.com/how-to-study-in-college-walter-paulk-manual/

*Parents' guide to transition.* (2009, February 4). Retrieved from http://www.heath.gwu.edu/index.php?option=com_content&task=view&id=1093&Itemid=56 [This article provides much information on transition planning and a thorough explanation of the differences in the laws governing colleges and those governing the public schools.]

Prochaska, J. O., Norcross, J. C., & DiClemente, C. C. (1994). *Changing for good: A revolutionary six-stage program for over-coming bad habits and moving your life positively forward.* New York, NY: William Morrow.

Roffman, A. (n.d.). *Tablespoons & teaspoons: Teaching teens with LD the art of meal preparation.* Retrieved from http://www. greatschools.org/LD/school-learning/tablespoons-and-teaspoons-teaching-teens-with-ld-the-art-of-meal-preparation.gs?content=926

Rosengren, C. (2005, October 27). *Changing your behavior.* Retrieved from http://curtrosengren.typepad.com/ occupationaladventure/2005/10/changing_your_b.html

*Self-Advocacy.* (n.d.). Retrieved from http://www.heath.gwu.edu/ index.php?option=com_content&task=view&id=1055&Itemid=4 0 [In addition to explaining self-advocacy, this article explains the differences in the laws governing college and those governing the public schools and the important role of the young adult in obtaining accommodations and services.]

Strichart, S. S. & Magrum II, C. T. (2002). *Teaching learning strategies and study skills to students with learning disabilities, at-tention deficit disorders or special needs, third edition.* Boston, MA: Allyn and Bacon.

Walter, T. L., Siebert, A., & Smith, L. N. (2000). *Student success: How to succeed in college and still have time for your friends.* Orlando, FL: Harcourt Brace & Company.

U.S. Department of Education, Office for Civil Rights. (2007, September). *Students with disabilities preparing for postsecondary education: Know your rights and responsibilities.* Retrieved from http://www.ed.gov/about/offices/list/ocr/transition.html

## Additional Online Resources for Teens

HEATH Resource Center: The HEATH Resource Center is an online clearinghouse on postsecondary education for individuals with disabilities (http://www.heath.gwu.edu).

*Strengthsquest* is an online survey that assesses talents and interests (https://www.strengthsquest.com/).

For videos, http://going-to-college.org has links to learning style surveys, materials for students, teachers and parents to assist in preparing for and transitioning to college.

Audiobooks are available at *Recordings for the Blind and Dyslexic:* http://www.rfbd.org/or

*Bookshare* is an electronic library for people with print disabilities: http://www.bookshare.org/

Also you might try *Natural Reader* http://www.naturalreaders.com/?gclid=CMWo4KWIsaACFYha2god5BxETA or *Read Please:* http://www.readplease.com/

Dictation Software can be found at *Dragon Naturally Speaking Nuance:* http://shop.nuance.com

## Coaching Resources

Information on training and finding a coach can be found at the International Coach Federation website (http://www.coachfederation.org) and the Coaches Training Institute website (http://www.thecoaches.com).

# About the Authors

THERESA E. LAURIE MAITLAND is currently the coordinator of the Academic Success Program for Students with LD/ADHD, which is a program in the Learning Center at the University of North Carolina at Chapel Hill. She has been on the staff at UNC-CH since 1994. It is Dr. Maitland's passion to work with individuals with learning, attention and emotional challenges so they can turn those challenges into gifts. Since 1996 Dr. Maitland and her colleagues at UNC have been studying the field of professional coaching and its application to college students with special learning needs. As a result, in 2003 she became a certified professional co-active coach (CPCC).

Prior to joining the staff at UNC, she worked as a special class teacher at all grade levels, a college professor, an in-service trainer, and a clinician. In 1984, Dr. Maitland helped develop a unique, private, multidisciplinary clinic for individuals with cognitive, emotional and behavioral challenges and their families. Throughout her career, Dr. Maitland has conducted numerous local and national presentations on topics related to teaching and parenting children, adolescents and young adults with these challenges. Dr. Maitland has a private practice that allows her to function as a professional coach and a consultant who specializes in issues related to the preparation of individuals with learning differences for life after high school. She has coauthored a book titled *Coaching College Students With ADHD: Issues and Answers* with Dr. Patricia Quinn and Nancy Ratey.

PATRICIA O. QUINN, MD, is a developmental pediatrician with over 30 years experience in private practice in Washington, DC. In 1997, she cofounded the National Center for Girls and Women with AD/HD, where she is currently director.

Dr. Quinn is a well-known international speaker and conducts workshops nationwide about attention-deficit/hyperactivity disorder (ADHD), and has authored several best-selling and groundbreaking books on the topic. In the last decade, she has devoted her attention professionally to the issues confronting girls and women with ADD (ADHD) with a particular interest on the relationship of a mother and child with ADHD. She also feels a strong commitment to working with teenagers and college students with ADHD, helping them to identify and manage issues specific to their age group. In 2000, Dr. Quinn received the Children and Adults With Attention-Deficit/Hyperactivity Disorder (CHADD) Hall of Fame Award.

## About Magination Press

Magination Press publishes self-help books for kids and the adults in their lives. Magination Press is an imprint of the American Psychological Association, the largest scientific and professional organization representing psychologists in the United States and the largest association of psychologists worldwide.